the Ulster Covenant

the Ulster Covenant

An Illustrated History of the 1912 Home Rule Crisis

Gordon Lucy

First published 1989 by
New Ulster (Publications) Ltd

This edition published 2012 by Colourpoint Books
An imprint of Colourpoint Creative Ltd
Colourpoint House, Jubilee Business Park
21 Jubilee Road, Newtownards, BT23 4YH
Tel: 028 9182 6339
Fax: 028 9182 1900
E-mail: info@colourpoint.co.uk
Web: www.colourpoint.co.uk

First Edition
First Impression

A catalogue record for this book is available from the British Library.

Designed by April Sky Design, Newtownards
Tel: 028 9182 7195
Web: www.aprilsky.co.uk

Printed by GPS Colour Graphics, Belfast

ISBN 978-1-78073-039-4

Front cover: The vast crowds gathered at Belfast City Hall on Ulster Day. *(PRONI INF7A/2/37)*
Inset: Carson poses for photographers while signing the Covenant. *(PRONI INF7A/2/47)*
Rear cover: An artist's impression of Donegall Place, Belfast, under Home Rule. *(Grand Orange Lodge of Ireland archive)*
Frontispiece: Carson in familiar pose speaking at outdoor rally. *(PRONI INF7A/2/84)*

CONTENTS

PREFACE

THIS YEAR WE EMBARK ON what is widely described as 'A Decade of Centenaries', a development which some will welcome and others deplore. In a volume of papers, entitled *Gladstone: Ireland and Beyond* (Dublin, 2011) to mark the bicentenary of the birth of William Ewart Gladstone, the author of the first and second Home Rule bills, Theodore Hoppen, Emeritus Professor of History in the University of Hull, observes:

> "Anniversaries, especially when expressed in large and round numbers, lie close to the human heart, in part at least because – whether for individuals, nations, religions or organizations – they help connect the past with the present."

Neil MacGregor, the Director of the British Museum, in his much admired *History of the World in 100 Objects* (London, 2010) deplores the modern obsession with centenaries and bicentenaries:

> "You can hardly turn on the radio or open a newspaper without being bombarded by yet another anniversary – a hundred years since this, two hundred since that. Our popular history seems to be written increasingly in centenaries, all generating books and exhibitions, T-shirts and special souvenir issues, in a frenzy of commemoration."

However, in his thoughtful consideration of a woodblock print, from Leipzig, MacGregor explains that the first of these modern centenary celebrations would appear to have taken place in Saxony in October 1617 to mark the centenary of the beginning of the Reformation.

For good or ill, over the next decade unionists and nationalists will celebrate, commemorate or mark the centenaries of a wide variety of events. The first significant anniversary is of the signing of the Ulster Covenant and Women's Declaration on 28 September 1912, the focus of this book.

The events of the decade 1912-1922 have had a disproportionate impact in shaping the course of Ulster, Irish and British history. These anniversaries ought not to be feared but embraced as opportunities to learn more about the past, to reflect soberly on those events and to evaluate their significance. Above all, these anniversaries afford us the opportunity to explore the complex relationship between the past and the present and to contemplate the challenging relationship between the past and the future. This publication is a contribution to that process.

As Dr Brian Young of Christ Church, Oxford, shrewdly notes in the *University of Oxford History Faculty Alumni Newsletter No. 3* (May 2005):

> "Talk of centenaries can make past events seem more than usually distant, and the whole notion of commemorating them can have the effect of memorialising rather than critically assessing such moments. One way of ensuring that assessment prevails over commemoration is to consider just how short a time one hundred years actually is."

Gordon Lucy, 2012

PRELUDE

TO THE UNIONISTS OF ULSTER the Solemn League and Covenant of 1912 is an Article of Faith. Signatories and their descendants alike held and hold it with a reverence akin to that of Englishmen for Magna Carta and Americans for the Declaration of Independence. It achieved that exalted status simply because for them it spoke of the highest values cherished by a freedom-loving people.

Theirs was no declaration of independence (indeed it was actually a statement of unswerving loyalty to the State), however it foreshadowed an earnest intent; Ulster unionists would mould their own destiny rather than permit a Government to filch away their birthright and dilute their citizenship by what they perceived as its unprincipled and unscrupulous activities. The Covenant and the resolutions accompanying it were a testimony to the indomitable spirit of Ulster's unionists: their feelings echoed the sentiments of Gustavus Hamilton (the Governor of Enniskillen) in 1688: "We stand upon our guard and do resolve, by the blessing of God, rather to meet our danger than to await it."

For the leaders of Ulster Unionism, the Covenant marked a further step in their determination to prevent the establishment of rule from Dublin. Home Rule, they were convinced, would be economically disastrous for the whole of Ireland, would constrain their citizenship and would inhibit the freedoms of all Irishmen. This document, and the oath enshrined within it, captured all the essential elements in their campaign, and those who framed it aimed to persuade the people of the United Kingdom to act to prevent the unjust, and seemingly inevitable, destruction of the Union between Great Britain and Ireland. Both islands had prospered under this Union, and Ulster unionists unreservedly believed that when mainland opinion was awakened to the deceit contemplated by the current administration, the desire for fair play would so manifest itself as to make that regime think again. However, the Covenant also sounded a note of warning: of an inevitable, violent outcome should the Government not stop its scheming.

The Covenant was a call to unionism's men and women to demonstrate their resolve; and it was a call which found a ready response. Thereafter the fate of unionist people and their leaders were inextricably bound together. The Covenant, by mobilising the people, strengthened the bonds of solidarity and instilled the necessary discipline to offer coherent opposition. It was, furthermore, a challenge to the Liberal Government to desist from its current and, for unionists, unprincipled and unjust intentions. It was a loud and clear commitment by Unionists that they would not surrender their heritage: unionists did not desire conflict with government, however, if it were forced upon them they would meet the threat. Their solemn oath marked the pinnacle of reasoned resistance. If the Government persisted in altering the law of the land, attacking basic freedoms, unionists would stand firm in the defence of their position.

Unionists knew well that they were entering upon a great crisis which would determine their destruction or survival as a free people within the United Kingdom. The Covenant was an expression of their will to survive.

However it went further – in effect, the Covenant was a three-fold challenge: a challenge to cynical politicians to desist from their folly; a challenge to the British public to concede the justice of Ulster's cause; and a challenge to unionist men and women to fulfil the obligations they had undertaken.

Between 1295 and 1800, Ireland had its own Parliament. Although subject to considerable control from London, it asserted a greater degree of independence in the last decades of the eighteenth century during the reign of George III. However, the savage anarchy of the 1798 rebellion so alarmed the British government that it decided to abolish the Irish Parliament.

The British Government favoured the idea of Union as a means of uniting the Protestants and Roman Catholics of Ireland. By transferring their representation to Westminster it was believed that these two traditions would be brought closer together. The Act of Union was duly passed on 1 August 1800, becoming effective on the first day of the following year.

As the new century progressed the beneficial effects of the Union became manifest. Politicians from Ireland found that their views and decisions had a much wider influence – they occupied a place on the world stage, not merely in some provincial sideshow. Moreover, the economics of both countries were closely interwoven and industry benefitted, especially in Ulster, from access to Britain's expanding markets. In effect, the citizens of Ireland reaped all the rewards of living under the British Constitution.

However, the fact that Ulster was the only part of the island to experience the full vigour of the Industrial Revolution set the province apart from the overwhelmingly agricultural south and west of the island. Unionists believed not only that Belfast and its environs flourished economically under the Union but also that they flourished because of the Union.

As early as 1834 Emerson Tennent, who was one of Belfast's two MPs, eloquently countered Daniel O'Connell's speech in the House of Commons in favour of repeal of the Union with the observation: "The north of Ireland had, every five years, found its trade doubled since the Union." In 1841 the Rev Dr Henry Cooke similarly repudiated O'Connell's case for repeal of the Union by recourse to Belfast's experience under the Union:

> "Look at the town of Belfast. When I myself was a youth I remember it almost a village. But what a glorious sight does it now present – the masted grove within our harbour – our mighty warehouses teeming with the wealth of every climate – our giant manufactories lifting themselves on every side – our streets marching on, as it were, with such rapidity that an absence of a few weeks makes us strangers in the outskirts of our town. And all this we owe to the Union... In one word more, I have done. Look at Belfast and be a Repealer, if you can."

When the Union came under threat from the mid 1880s onwards, Belfast Chamber of Commerce played an important role in combating what became known as the 'Home Rule' threat. The Chamber stressed that Ulster's wealth and prosperity was due to the "security and protection" afforded by parliament since the Act of Union and the "frugality and enterprise" of its people.

By the end of the nineteenth century Belfast was part of an industrial complex that stretched from Lancashire to Lanarkshire. In 1911 Philip Cambrai described Belfast as "one of the biggest, most energetic and commercially successful cities of the Empire." By 1914 Belfast could boast "the greatest shipyard, rope works, tobacco factory, linen mill, dry dock and tea machinery works in the world." In the late nineteenth and early twentieth centuries Belfast was one of the major industrial powerhouses of the world.

Ulster Unionists believed that Ulster's prosperity would be jeopardised by Home Rule. Unionists believed that nationalists would raise tariff barriers and so provoke retaliatory tariffs that would impede or exclude Ulster exports from overseas markets. Unionists believed that the overwhelmingly agricultural south and west would be unsympathetic to Ulster's industrial and commercial interests. They also feared that Ulster would be over-taxed, and that Ulster would end up shouldering the burden of a Home Rule parliament's profligate expenditure.

Not everyone in Ireland, however, was satisfied with the blessings bestowed by the Union. Irish Nationalists wanted to set up a new Parliament in Dublin with increased powers. The movement in favour of independent government gained momentum as the century progressed and became increasingly aligned with the Roman Catholic Church, especially following the granting of 'Catholic Emancipation' in 1829 and the expanding power of the Church from 1850.

The movement for Home Rule also took the form of agitation over various real and imaginary grievances which affected Irish life. Whereas in Britain such problems were seen to be economic and social, in Ireland, the Nationalists saw them as political, especially in the vexed area of land ownership.

An artist's impression of a Land League demonstration at Limerick.
(Grand Orange Lodge of Ireland archive)

Thus it was that questions of religious persuasion and economic standing came to be superimposed on the whole constitutional issue and increased the divide between the largely Roman Catholic and agrarian South and the predominantly Protestant and industrial North. In the 1870s and 1880s the extravagant language of the Home Rule movement gave rise to increased violence, thus Ulster unionists considered that they had had a glimpse of the reality of a future Dublin Parliament.

While the illustration above depicts a comparatively orderly Land League meeting, Unionists equated the League with murder, intimidation and agrarian violence, the ugly and inhumane face of the Home Rule movement.

Rudyard Kipling's poem 'Cleared', prompted by publication of the Report of the Parnell Commission, succinctly sets the Unionist case. In 1887 and 1888 *The Times* had published articles, entitled "Parnellism and Crime," linking CS Parnell, the Nationalist leader, with involvement in criminal conspiracy and murder. In February 1890 the Parnell Commission, established by the Conservative Government, reported and found that the letters published by *The Times* were forgeries and exonerated Parnell of all serious charges. Although the headline news was that Parnell was innocent, the Report named seven prominent Nationalist MPs, including Davitt, Dillon and O'Brien, who had taken part in activities which "led to crime and outrage and persisted in it with knowledge of its effects." Kipling's poem sought to focus on the latter point:

> If black is black or white is white, in black and white it's down,
>
> You're only traitors to the Queen and rebels to the Crown.
>
> If print is print or words are words, the learned court perpends,
>
> We are not ruled by murderers, but only – by their friends.

Unionists regarded the Land League as a threat which was both economic and political. The League's methods convinced them that Irish Home Rule would inevitably result in injustice, economic ruin and anarchy. Their view was that irresponsible Irish Nationalists had thus forfeited the chance of self-government. For the good of all, the Union must be preserved.

Unionists believed that any new Dublin Parliament would be predominantly Roman Catholic, and unduly influenced by that Church – hence the popular slogan "Home Rule is Rome Rule" – and that freedom of religious practice for Protestants would soon be drastically curtailed. The slogan dates from the 1870s and may have been coined by John Bright, the radical Quaker and MP, who had been one of the architects of the Anti-Corn Law League. To the unionists of Ulster it was not bigotry to try to prevent the setting-up of a parliament of bigots.

Henry Cooke, The Father of Ulster Unionism.

In an age when religious affiliation frequently determined political allegiance in Britain, the Unionist campaign against Dublin rule had the familiar ring of a religious crusade – one for the defence of Protestantism.

Many of these politico-religious themes had earlier come together in the person of the outstanding Presbyterian cleric, whom we have already encountered, Henry Cooke (whose statue, commonly known as 'The Black Man', stands outside the Royal Belfast Academical Institution, College Square East, Belfast). At a great meeting in Hillsborough in October 1834, Cooke had stood out to preserve Protestantism from nationalist onslaughts by declaring a new era of Protestant co-operation. The emphasis on a common Protestantism rather than denominationalism proved an enduring bond which assumed, then and later, an immense political, as well as religious significance.

In this role, pursued throughout his life, Cooke carved out for himself a place as one of the Founding Fathers of Unionism. The Archdeacon of Connor, in 1888 declared that Cooke was above all a patriot: he understood that Repeal of the Union meant more than the dissolution of the bonds between Ireland and England – it meant dismemberment of the Empire, a reduction in the United Kingdom's world status, and destruction of Ireland's commerce and her civil and religious liberties. Cooke's firm convictions were eagerly emulated and admired by succeeding generations of Unionists.

From the mid-1880s, two factors prompted Unionists to organize themselves as a more coherent lobby: fear of Nationalist influence in Britain, and a growing pride in Ulster's contribution to the United Kingdom's greatness. Long-standing demarcation lines between the political parties were blurred as Unionists of Liberal and Conservative backgrounds sank their differences in a common opposition to a Dublin Parliament.

Unionists in Great Britain and Ireland co-operated to defeat the Home Rule Bills proposed by the Liberal Prime Minister, Gladstone first in 1886 and again in 1893. The views of Ulster Unionists were forcefully summed up by

An artist's impression of the Ulster Unionist Convention of 17 June 1892. *(Grand Orange Lodge of Ireland archive)*

Lord Salisbury, leader of the Conservative Party, when he declared that "Parliament has a right to govern the people of Ulster; it has not a right to sell them into slavery."

Events such as the Ulster Unionist Convention of June, 1892, when 20,000 people, including democratically elected delegates from all over the Province, assembled in Belfast, demonstrated to the world that Ulster Unionists were resolved never to surrender to Dublin rule, and ever to defend their equal rights within the United Kingdom.

The view inside the huge purpose-built hall, at Stranmillis in Belfast, constructed for the Ulster Unionist Convention. *(PRONI INF7A/1/6)*

The first Home Rule Bill was defeated in the House of Commons in June 1886; the second met the same fate in the House of Lords in September 1893; but the state of British party politics in the new century made it almost certain that a third attempt would be made. As a result of the two general elections of January and December 1910 the Liberal Government could only stay in office with Irish Nationalist support; the price was yet another Home Rule Bill. The Parliament Act of 1911 deprived the House of Lords, a bulwark of the Union in 1893, of its veto. Short of a general election before 1914, the Bill was certain to reach the statute book.

COPYRIGHT.   BAIRD, BELFAST.

DONEGALL PLACE, BELFAST, UNDER HOME RULE.

(Grand Orange Lodge of Ireland archive)

Unionists knew that Ireland had fared infinitely better under Westminster than she could hope to do under a Dublin Parliament. They refused to alter a system under which Ireland prospered. There were several excellent reasons for their view, the major ones being the belief that any weakening of the Union would retard economic progress, curtail religious liberty and imperil civil rights. As FE Smith said, it was a contest "between parochialism and Imperialism; between ultra-montanism and religious liberty; it is between stagnation and progress."

It was the deep conviction of Unionists that Dublin rule would be ruinous to the prosperity of Ulster, a view

BELFAST UNDER HOME RULE.   Making a Site for the Statue of King John the First of Ireland.

(Grand Orange Lodge of Ireland archive)

epitomised in an artist's impression of Donegall Place under Home Rule (page 13). Belfast's prestigious City Hall, token of Ulster's civic pride, and symbolic of her kinship with Great Britain (being on a par with the civic splendour of public buildings in mainland industrial cities), now lies derelict; the primary commercial premises, so long a testament to the Ulster businessman's entrepreneurial spirit, are vacant and neglected; and the once-crowded thoroughfares, representative of a hard-working, energetic people, are now overgrown and serve only as rough pasture for a few bedraggled beasts of the field.

A second postcard (page 14) depicts the demolition of the Albert Clock, erected as a memorial to the Prince Consort, Queen Victoria's husband who died in 1861, and its replacement with a statue of John Redmond, the Nationalist leader. Equally significant are the busy 'Protestant Emigration Office' and the full Poor House, denoting that Protestants would have no place in a Home Rule Ireland and that poverty would be the order of the day.

Similar postcards exist depicting the impact of Home Rule on both Lisburn and Portadown.

Unionists, proud of Ulster's contribution to the United Kingdom's role as workshop of the world, felt Home Rule would deprive it of access to the markets of the British Empire. The three successive Home Rule crises served only to highlight the economic differences between the industrial North and the agrarian South and West.

Unionism was based on a belief in the British system of government embodying justice and fair play. Echoing the Archdeacon of Connor's judgement of Henry Cooke, Unionists considered themselves true patriots. To them the founding of a Dublin parliament would signal the end of an administrative order which had carried the United Kingdom to pre-eminence amongst the nations. This sentiment was most vividly demonstrated in the manner in which the Union was revered.

The watchwords of Unionism such as 'loyalty', 'duty', 'service', 'integrity' and 'self-sacrifice', were held to be the very elements which served to make Britain great. Britain's pre-eminent position in the world was evidenced by the magnitude of her Empire; the Union Flag flew over 400 million people and more than a quarter of the world map was coloured red. Opponents of Home Rule were not slow to point out their part in establishing this Empire, as soldiers, diplomats, missionaries, financiers and businessmen.

Yet, despite their devotion to the Crown, Parliament and the law, Unionists conveyed to those in power that their loyalty was not blind. Indeed, as the Third Home Rule crisis developed, it became clear that Ulster Loyalists, regarding the Constitution as sacrosanct, would not merely toe the line of any particular British Government. In their view, the Liberal Administration was acting outside the Constitution by attempting to deprive Ireland of her place under the Westminster Parliament. Thus, they had a right, indeed a duty, to resist, although they had no desire to flout the law. As Sir Edward Carson said:

> "It is you (the Government) who are prepared to break the law, and it is I who am prepared to resist you when you break it."

This opposition was based on a desire to uphold integration with Great Britain, but it implied that independence would be chosen as the final alternative to rule from Dublin.

DEMONSTRATIONS

WITH THEIR RIGHTS THREATENED BY 'a parliamentary dictatorship' created solely by the Liberal Government's desperate dependence on Irish Nationalist votes in Parliament, the Ulster Unionists were forced to resort to extra-parliamentary means to express their relentless opposition to Home Rule and to their being denied their full rights as British citizens. Unionists demonstrated that no one might think that their resolve had weakened, that their leaders no longer spoke for them when they warned that Ulster would resist.

Unionists exhibited real flair and organisational ability in staging impressive mass demonstrations on the scale

The grounds of Craigavon House, as the Orangemen and the members of the Unionist Clubs arrive. *(PRONI D961/3/001)*

Carson, Craig and the Unionist leadership pose for pictures in front of Craigavon House. *(PRONI D961/1/004)*

of those held at Craigavon on 23 September 1911 and at Balmoral on 9 April 1912. The former was organised by Captain James Craig, the Unionist MP for East Down, while the latter was organised by a sub-committee, chaired by Sir James Henderson, the proprietor of the *Belfast News Letter*.

With respect to the Craigavon demonstration, held in the grounds of James Craig's home in east Belfast, the Liberal Unionist *Northern Whig* opined that it was "the largest demonstration ever mustered in Belfast", surpassing even the Ulster Unionist Convention of 17 June 1892. The Conservative *Belfast News Letter* estimated that at least 100,000 people, drawn from the Unionist Clubs and the Orange Order, were present. Historians usually prefer to put the audience at 50,000. Unionist Clubs had been established to provide Unionism with a local network, but they became moribund when the Home Rule threat disappeared, especially after the return of a Unionist Government in July 1895. With the renewal of that threat, towards the end of 1910 the Ulster Unionist Council asked Lord Templetown to revive the organisation. He

Templepatrick Unionist Club at the Balmoral Demonstration, from *The Graphic* 13 April 1912. *(PRONI INF7A/2/12)*

had founded the first Unionist Club at his home, Castle Upton, Templepatrick, Co Antrim in 1893 at the height of the second Home Rule crisis. His Templepatrick Unionist Club was therefore known as "the premier Unionist Club," because it was the first to be formed. By mid-December 1911 there were 164 Clubs in existence. In all 139 Unionist Clubs were represented at the Craigavon Demonstration in September 1911. By the end of February 1912 there were 232 Clubs.

Sir Edward Carson's speech was the highlight of the day's events. He told his audience that he was entering into "a compact, or bargain," with them. He continued:

"with the help of God, you and I joined together – I giving the best I can, and you giving all your strength behind me – we will yet defeat the most nefarious conspiracy [Home Rule] that has ever been hatched against a free people."

As a covenant is a bargain or agreement, this passage could be viewed as anticipating Ulster's Solemn League and Covenant.

Carson offered "an admirably lucid and forceful" statement of the Unionist position:

"Our demand is a very simple one. We ask for no privileges, but we are determined that no one shall have privileges over us. We ask for no special rights, but we claim the same rights from the same Government as every other part of the United Kingdom. We ask for nothing more; we will take nothing less. It is our inalienable right as citizens of the British Empire, and Heaven help the men who will try and take it from us."

In the crucial passage of his speech, Carson told the assembled multitudes at Craigavon:

"We must be prepared ... the morning Home Rule passes, ourselves to become responsible for the government of the Protestant Province of Ulster."

Carson's aim was the comprehensive defeat of Home Rule. He believed that Home Rule was not economically viable without Ulster's, and more specifically Belfast's, heavy industry and that John Redmond, the Nationalist leader, and Irish Nationalist opinion would never accept Home Rule with Ulster exclusion. Therefore, Carson was convinced that if he could demonstrate that Ulster Unionists were resolute in their determination to oppose Home Rule, Home Rule would be "dead as a stone." Therefore, this provides the context for Carson's statement.

Liberals and Nationalists variously ignored, discounted and dismissed Carson's speech as 'bluff and bluster'. For example, leading Liberal politicians, members of the 'Eighty Club', were visiting Ireland on a 'fact-finding' mission but these 'political tourists' declined an invitation to attend and observe the proceedings.

Jeremiah McVeagh, a journalist and Nationalist MP for South Down, contended: "Ulster will bluster but will not fight". In October 1911, Winston Churchill, then a Liberal cabinet minister, in a speech to his Dundee constituents, said: "I daresay when the worst comes to the worst we shall find that civil war evaporates in uncivil words."

The success of the Craigavon Demonstration was surpassed by that held on 9 April 1912, on the eve of the introduction of the Home Rule Bill in Parliament, when masses of vehicles and nearly 70 special trains brought Unionists into Belfast. In all 200,000 Unionists gathered at the showgrounds of the North-East Agricultural Association at Balmoral, including huge contingents of Orangemen and Unionist Clubs members who marched in formation both from Dunmurry, County Antrim, and the city centre. All the Orange Lodges and Unionist Clubs displayed Union Flags and some banners as they marched. Their demonstration was boosted by the presence of a large body of English and Scottish Tory MPs, most notably the new Tory leader, Andrew Bonar Law.

Law and Carson were the principal speakers. The Church of Ireland Primate of All Ireland and the Moderator of the Presbyterian Church conducted a religious service. Their presence contributed to the solemnity of the occasion.

Law told the vast crowd that their cause was no narrow provincial protest but the cause of the Empire, and praised them for "a fixity of resolution which nothing can shake and which must prove irresistible." In his opinion, there were two peoples in Ireland separated by "a gulf of race and religion"; one loyal to King and Empire and the other regarding even the display of the Union Flag as an insult.

Carson told the Demonstration: "We have one object in view, and that is the object of victory, and we are going to win." He warned the Government: "As you have treated us with fraud, if necessary we will treat you with force."

At the conclusion of his speech, Carson invited every one present to raise their hands and repeat after him: "Never under any circumstances will we submit to Home

The leaders' platform at the Balmoral Demonstration featuring Bonar Law and Carson (centre, both holding their hats). *(PRONI INF7A/2/11)*

Medals marking the 1892 Ulster Unionist Convention and the 1912 Demonstration. *(Grand Orange Lodge of Ireland archive)*

Rule." Law joined Carson in raising his hand and repeating Carson's pledge.

Carson's dramatic gesture, at the conclusion of Law's speech, prompted an idea in the minds of some of the Unionist leadership of an oath or a pledge to be taken by the entire unionist population. Therein, lay the immediate origins of the Ulster Covenant.

The presence of Bonar Law, the Tory leader since November 1911 (standing on Carson's right in the photograph), gave a massive boost to the Ulster Unionists' morale and emphasised his acceptance of a vital element in British history, namely the citizen's right to oppose an unjust imposition by any Government.

There was a strong personal dimension to Law's support for Ulster, as he was steeped in its culture and heritage. Although Law was born in Kingston, New Brunswick (one of the maritime provinces of modern Canada), and largely grew up in Glasgow and its environs, his father, Rev James Law, was a Presbyterian minister from Coleraine. His brother, William, was a much-respected physician in Coleraine. In 1877, Rev James Law returned to live at Maddybenny, near Coleraine, and died there in 1882. During the last five years of his father's life, despite being a notoriously bad sailor, the then Glasgow-based Law visited Ulster almost every weekend to see his father. Law knew Ulster and her people well. His sympathies were with Ulster Unionism.

The Unionists ensured that the full propaganda value was obtained from Bonar Law's presence and from the whole demonstration. Newspaper reporters were provided with telegraph facilities and a special observation platform gave photographers an uninterrupted view of the leaders and of the crowd.

3

THE COVENANT CAMPAIGN

IGNORING THE WARNINGS FROM ULSTER'S elected representatives and from the Conservative Opposition in Parliament, the British Government, needing Irish Nationalist votes to stay in power, pressed ahead with its plan to impose Home Rule – Dublin rule – on Ulster. Carson feared the consequences of London's schemes in Ulster; mounting tension between Unionists and Nationalists, violent incidents leading to further violent incidents, the dreadful slide into full-scale civil war and the inevitable loss of innocent lives.

Determined to resist Home Rule but also to contain the dangers created by Nationalist and British Government pressures, Carson endorsed a series of eleven meetings held over ten days, the famous 'Covenant Campaign' of September 1912 organised by James Craig.

From Enniskillen to Londonderry, from Ballymena to Portadown, from Coleraine to the last great rally at the Ulster Hall, Belfast, on 27 September, Carson addressed meetings of thousands of Unionists. Everywhere his listeners were called upon to bestir themselves and order the affairs of a people in the grave crisis which threatened to engulf them. Everywhere that clear message was accompanied by an equally clear call to maintain order and discipline. Thus at the first great meeting at Enniskillen, chosen for its symbolic significance as the western gateway to Ulster, 30-40,000 Unionist Club members, with two mounted squadrons of Volunteers, marched past the Unionist leader in immaculate order. The town set the tone for all the later demonstrations, exhibiting the people's mixture of solemn determination

Carson in Great Victoria Street railway station, Belfast, before setting out for Enniskillen, the first pre-Covenant demonstration. The stationmaster asked Carson to inform his counterpart at Clones railway station: "We will not have Home Rule!" *(Grand Orange Lodge of Ireland archive)*

The Enniskillen Horse at the Enniskillen Demonstration, 18 September 1912. *(PRONI D2638/E/16)*

and confident enthusiasm for the Campaign.

This photograph above shows the mounted Yeomanry, formed by William Copeland Trimble, the editor of The *Impartial Reporter,* which provided Carson's escort as they headed the march to Portora Hill. It was a display which both emphasised the Ulstermen's readiness to fight if forced to defend themselves and evoked the glorious role of Enniskillen in standing against James II's forces during

the 'Glorious Revolution' and thus contributing to the struggle for civil and religious liberty.

Special trains from Belturbet, Cootehill, Bundoran, Monaghan, Castleblayney, Omagh, and many other towns brought Unionists to the Enniskillen Demonstration. Enniskillen, recognising the honour bestowed on it, festooned its streets with bunting and flags, and erected an impressive number of arches.

"WE WILL NOT HAVE HOME RULE"
THE OPENING MEETING AT ENNISKILLEN OF THE GREAT ULSTER CAMPAIGN

Thirty thousand people took part in the inaugural meeting at Enniskillen of the great campaign against Home Rule, which culminates to-day (Saturday) in the signing of the Solemn Covenant of resistance throughout Ulster. Presiding on the platform was the Earl of Erne, who opened the meeting. He was followed by Sir Edward Carson, the brilliant leader of the great movement, who made a fighting speech, resolute and fervent in tone, listened to by the vast audience on the hillside beside Lough Erne with rapt attention, and cheered again and again, with tremendous shouts of "We will not have Home Rule."

The Enniskillen Demonstration, 18 September 1912. *(PRONI D2638/E/16)*

The *Daily Graphic's* report of Carson at the Enniskillen Demonstration in its edition of 20 September 1912. *(PRONI D1479/2/13)*

The photograph on the left on page 23 shows the elderly Earl of Erne opening the proceedings. The highlight was a forceful speech by Carson in which he leaves his audience in no doubt as to what they might be called upon to do in the near future. The road offered was that of sacrifice; the same road that he and the other Unionist leaders were prepared to take. Together they must prove, he warned them, that they were not decadent sons of their glorious ancestors.

Enniskillen's example was followed everywhere else. The whole Unionist population was to be mobilised to meet any eventuality. No doubt was to be left in London or in Dublin that Ulster men and women were equally determined to resist a perceived grave political injustice.

The second pre-Covenant rally took place in the Grain Market in Lisburn and attracted an estimated 20,000 people.

Carson took great pains to emphasise to his audience that their quarrel was the Liberal Government rather than their Roman Catholic or nationalist neighbours: "Always remember our quarrel is not with any individuals; our quarrel is with the Government, and with the Government we mean to carry out this quarrel to the end..." James Craig MP during his speech amusingly observed that "there were two sides to every argument except Home Rule in Lisburn".

Carson, responding to a vote of thanks, at the end the evening, said:

> "I go back strengthened in my resolve that both inside and outside the House of Commons I will do all that is possible with the strength God has given me to resist the policy of Home Rule. Now I say good-night, and God bless you."

Londonderry Demonstration of 20 September 1912, as depicted on the front page of *The Graphic*, 28 September 1912. *(Belfast Central Library Newspaper Archive)*

SIR EDWARD CARSON'S ENTHUSIASTIC ARMY OF UNIONISTS AT LONDONDERRY.

The great procession of Unionists crossing the Carlisle Bridge (later replaced by the Craigavon Bridge), Londonderry. *(PRONI D2638/E/16)*

The third demonstration of the Covenant Campaign was held in Londonderry. On his arrival at the railway station, Carson was provided with a guard of honour from the local Unionist Clubs and with a bodyguard of 100 men. Fife and flute bands preceded the four open carriages which conveyed the dignitaries through the streets vibrant with the colours of flags, banners and emblems to the Guildhall, the first demonstration held indoors.

The Guildhall was the venue for rousing speeches to a wildly enthusiastic audience. Probably the most interesting speech was made by FE Smith, a leading English Tory, who explained why, as an Englishman, he sided with Ulster in its struggle against Home Rule; the struggle of 1912 was the same as that of 1688, a struggle for rights.

On 21 September the Covenant campaign was taken to Coleraine. Accompanied by bands and with flags waving in the breeze, Carson and Smith marched through a town ablaze with red, white and blue flags and bunting. At

SOUTH LONDONDERRY
WE WILL NOT HAVE
HOME RULE

Carson and FE Smith marching to the Coleraine Demonstration,
21 September 1912. *(PRONI INF7A/2/19)*

the Demonstration, in the grounds of the Manor House, Carson told the gathered thousands that the Covenant Campaign was no ordinary campaign:

> "It is the soul of a nation fighting against injustice ... It is the protest of men that no gold can buy, the protest of men who will not allow themselves to be sold."

The Demonstration at Coleraine drew thousands of Unionists from Lough Neagh to the Foyle, from Fair Head to County Tyrone, all to hear the oratory of Carson and FE Smith. At the railway station, where he arrived from Londonderry, Carson was met by a guard of honour drawn from the Ulster Clubs. He made an impromptu speech denying that Unionists wanted to stir up sectarianism and offering to Nationalists the hand of friendship "for the good of the empire and the good of our common country," if only Home Rule were abandoned.

The photograph on the left shows Carson, with FE Smith on his left, marching to the demonstration. On Carson's right is HT Barrie, the MP for North Londonderry. The banner belonged to a large contingent of Loyalists from South Londonderry which had just arrived in Coleraine by special train.

The photograph on the right shows the huge crowd stretching from Killowen to the town centre and beyond. The banner across the street, with its clear political message, was well caught by the camera.

The meeting at Portadown attracted an attendance of at least 30,000, many of them conveyed to Portadown by a large number of special trains put on for the occasion by the Great Northern Railway Company. Carson travelled by the 11:00 train from Belfast and arrived in Portadown at 11:45. On his arrival Carson was presented with two addresses

Men from the district Orange Lodges marching to the Manor House grounds during the Coleraine Demonstration, 21 September 1912. *(PRONI INF7A/2/18)*

of welcome; one from Portadown Urban District Council and the other from North Armagh Unionist Association.

A number of features of the Portadown Demonstration are worthy of note.

After his arrival at Portadown Station, Carson was greeted by men who presented arms with their dummy rifles, evidence of the drilling which had been taken place under the auspices of the Orange Order and the Unionist Clubs since early 1911. He was also provided with a mounted escort of 50 men under the command of Mr Holt

Carson's mounted escort leading the procession from Portadown Station. *(PRONI INF7A/2/13)*

Waring JP of Waringstown.

Portadown was lavishly decorated with flags and bunting for the occasion, through which a large procession of bands, men armed with their dummy rifles, and nurses marched with Carson – as the Daily Mirror reported "The town... was smothered in Union Jacks".

There were also a group of nurses and an ambulance, evidence of the willingness of women to play a proactive role in the unfolding political crisis.

There were also two mock cannon or artillery pieces, made of wood and painted a steel grey. FE Smith exclaimed: "The battle is already won."

Portadown appropriately decorated for the occasion. *(PRONI D2638/E/16)*

Nurses feature at prominently in this photograph at the Portadown Demonstration. *(PRONI INF7A/2/16)*

The two mock cannon made of wood at the Portadown Demonstration. *(PRONI D2638/E/16)*

Mrs Smith wrote to her sisters:

"We all thought the dummy cannons were absurd. It was only at Portadown we had them. We none of us knew anything about them. We all said: 'How the Radicals will laugh!'"

No doubt the Liberals and Nationalists did laugh but the dummy rifles and cannons may be seen in retrospect as an earnest of their intention to acquire real weapons.

Carson was the principal speaker and at the conclusion of the proceedings he was presented with a blackthorn stick "to beat Home Rule with."

Carson had intended to attend the demonstration at Ballyroney, near Rathfriland, but at the last minute was obliged to send his apologies.

From the perspective of the twenty-first century, Ballyroney appears to have been a curious choice of venue for one of the pre-Covenant demonstrations. However, it was the perfect venue for a Unionist demonstration in South Down a century ago because it was an important railway junction. The station today is a private house and part of the platform is now a lawn. Otherwise it remains more or less in its original condition.

The principal speaker at Ballyroney was the Earl of Kilmorey, supported by Admiral Lord Charles Beresford MP (who was widely regarded as the very personification of

'A stick to beat Home Rule with' – Carson brandishing the blackthorn stick that was presented to him at Portadown. *(PRONI D2638/E/16)*

The Countess of Kilmorey at Ballyroney. *(PRONI D2638/E/16)*

John Bull), Lord Willoughby de Broke (the fox-hunting but cerebral peer who was described by George Dangerfield, the radical journalist, in *The Strange Death of Liberal England* as "a genial and sporting young peer, whose face bore a pleasing resemblance to the horse ... He had quite a gift for writing, thought clearly, and was not more than two hundred years behind his time") and Ronald McNeill MP (an Ulster Unionist representing the St Augustine's division of Kent since 1911, a former assistant editor of the *Encyclopaedia Britannica*, and the future author of *Ulster's Stand for Union*).

The illustration above depicts the Countess of Kilmorey waving a Union Flag to greet the assembled crowds. As Ellen Constance Baldock, daughter of Edward Holmes Baldock, the Conservative MP for Shrewsbury, she married the 3rd Earl of Kilmorey in 1881. Their marriage is a measure of the extent to which the local unionist political elite was fully integrated into the wider British political elite.

Part of the huge crowd at the Ulster Hall Demonstration, Belfast, 27 September 1912. *(PRONI INF7A/2/25)*

The temporary canopy stand erected outside at the Ulster Hall Demonstration, 27 September 1912. *(PRONI INF7A/2/26)*

IN TOKEN OF ULSTER'S VICTORY: THE BANNER THAT LED AT THE BOYNE

The Ulster Hall Demonstration, 27 September 1912, as depicted on the front page of *The Graphic*, 5 October 1912. *(Belfast Central Library Newspaper Archive)*

The Ulster Hall could not accommodate all the thousands of people who wanted to attend the last and the biggest rally of the Covenant Campaign. According to the *Northern Whig:*

"At four o'clock, three hours before the meeting began, there were already a sprinkling of enthusiasts in evidence, an hour later the building was more than half filled, and before six o'clock it was a case of standing room only, and very little of that."

An overflow meeting was held in Bedford Street. The street was packed as far as the eye could see in either direction.

A platform was specially erected for the speakers outside an upper window and from it Carson addressed the crowd below. Messages were read from prominent Tories, including Andrew Bonar Law and Arthur James Balfour, Law's predecessor as party leader, thus emphasizing that, in its defence of the unity of the United Kingdom and of the Empire, Ulster did not stand alone.

The photograph on page 33 offers a closer view of the Union-Flag-bedecked special platform. The neon sign blazed forth to the British Parliament, to Irish Nationalists, and to the world, the sentiment common to all Ulster Unionists: "We will not have Home Rule."

The highlight of the Ulster Hall Demonstration was the unfurling of the Boyne Standard, an ancient-looking yellow silk banner allegedly carried by an Ensign Watson before William of Orange at the Battle of the Boyne on 1 July 1690. Nationalists and Radicals hotly contended that the banner was not genuine. The *Irish News* poured scorn on the alleged origins of the flag:

> "If that flag ever saw the Battle of the Boyne, all we can say is that the man who manufactured it deserves undying fame for the strength and durability of the material."

The *Belfast News Letter* grasped the essential point when it referred to the banner as a symbol of the "preciousness of the heritage" of Ulstermen and an inspiration to fight to maintain British citizenship. Presented with Boyne Standard, Carson told the huge crowd: "May this flag ever float over a people that can boast of civil and religious liberty." There remains a mystery; where is the silk banner now?

A cartoon of Carson as Wellington, from *Punch* of 25 September 1912. It is entitled "Ulster will write" and is captioned: "General Carson: 'The pen (for the moment) is mightier than the sword. Up nibs, and at 'em!'" *(Belfast Central Library Newspaper Archive)*

Opposite: The Ulster Hall meeting – Carson stands in the centre; standing beside him is Lord Londonderry. Immediately behind Carson are John Gordon, KC, MP and Sir James Craig. Behind Craig is Sir Robert Kennedy, KCVO, of Cultra Manor (now the Ulster Folk Museum). On the right of Lord Londonderry are Ronald McNeill and the Duke of Abercorn. FE Smith is to Carson's left beside Robert J McMordie, QC, Lord Mayor of Belfast. To the right of the picture with a white beard is GS Reade of York Street Flax Spinning Company. *(PRONI INF7A/2/29)*

4

THE LEADERS

IF THE CAMPAIGN AGAINST THE Third Home Rule Bill was a campaign which captured the imagination of a people, it was also a movement fired by the leadership qualities and the example of those towering figures who identified with and shared in the trials and the fears, the hopes and the principles of ordinary folk. What might have degenerated into an ill-directed, frustrated and, ultimately, violent protest, shone forth to the rest of the United Kingdom, the Empire and the world as an example of what a disciplined and determined people could achieve if given thoughtful and unflinching leadership.

The Crisis of 1912 proved beyond any doubt that Ulster could summon to its cause a wide variety of skilled men; prominent aristocrats, wealthy businessmen, talented lawyers, able parliamentarians and devout clergymen. They were not absentee leaders. All were local, some even national, establishment figures. Although the obvious temptation for the political leaders may have been to bargain for personal interests or to accept the harsh political reality of the situation, throughout the period of campaign they presented a united front to Ulster Unionism, remaining invested in their central belief; their right, the people's right, to be treated in the same way as the British citizens of any other part of the United Kingdom.

Above all the events and the figures stood Carson, an experienced parliamentary and legal advocate. When the Government rejected a compromise protecting just four counties from Home Rule (the Agar-Robartes amendment of June 1912), Carson, realising that he had wrong-footed the Government, confidently stepped up his campaign

The leaders' signatures. *(Belfast Central Library Newspaper Archive)*

against a Dublin Parliament.

Carson's command of tactics, his powerful oratory, and his obvious sincerity won for him the confidence of the Conservative Party's leadership. The Tory leader, Bonar

Carson looks towards the assembled photographers at the historic moment of his signing the Covenant. Behind him to the right stands Craig, the hard-working organiser of the Covenant Campaign rallies. As Patrick Buckland has shrewdly observed, Craig possessed "in larger measure than most Ulster Unionists a marked administrative ability, ample reserves of determination, energy and patience and, surprisingly, an eye for the dramatic." The specially provided silver inkstand is clearly visible on the Union Flag-draped table. Behind Carson can be seen the controversial Boyne banner. *(PRONI INF7A/2/47)*

Law, paying tribute to the disciplined restraint of Ulster Loyalists, told the House of Commons,

> "These people have only been restrained by two reasons. They have been restrained by the wise leadership and the self-control displayed by my Right Hon. friend [Carson]."

The text of the Covenant saw in Home Rule a political thraldom which would undermine Ulster's industrial and commercial prosperity, while denying to present and future generations of Ulstermen "Our cherished position of equal citizenship in the United Kingdom." To meet the danger the signatories pledged themselves to join "in using all means which may be found necessary," and that meant even the use of force.

As leader of the Ulster Unionists, Carson was the first to sign. Lord Londonderry representing the aristocracy and gentry, came next. The vital contributions of the Churches and of the Christian faith were recognised by the prominence given to the signatures of notable Churchmen. Despite his powerful position in the protest movement, Craig modestly did not claim any special place in the order of signing. Carson afterwards candidly admitted: "It was James Craig who did most of the work, and I got most of the credit."

The Duke of Abercorn, who had chaired the Ulster Unionist Convention protesting against Home Rule in 1892, two decades later was again involved in the campaign against a Parliament in Dublin. In failing health and too ill to travel, the Duke attended a service in the little church on his Baronscourt estate and was the first to sign the Covenant in the churchyard after the service. Perhaps it was intentionally symbolic that he sat under a sturdy oak

The Duke of Abercorn, KG, President of the Ulster Unionist Council, signing the Solemn League and Covenant on Ulster Day 1912 at Baronscourt, Co Tyrone. *(PRONI D2618/A/A/5)*

tree since, however frail his body, the Duke remained as determined as ever in spirit. The Duchess was the first to sign to the Women's Declaration. The Duke expressed himself delighted with large number of farmers present

FE Smith addressing a Unionist demonstration. *(PRONI INF7A/2/22)*

"considering the busy season and the favourable harvest weather."

FE Smith was one of the most prominent English Conservative supporters of the Ulster Unionist position. In the years before the Great War Frederick Edwin Smith was viewed as a future leader of his party and a future Prime Minister. Before he was 40 in July 1912 he had amassed a fortune at the Bar, had entered the House of Commons in 1906 as Conservative MP for Liverpool Walton, had taken silk in 1908 and had become a Privy

Councillor in 1911. Determined to make a name for himself in the Commons, as he had done in the Oxford Union and on the Northern Circuit, on 12 March 1906 FE Smith had defied the convention that maiden speeches are short, polite, modest and unprovocative. "When he rose to speak, he was unknown. When he sat down his reputation was made." "Who is this Effie Smith?" one elderly lady is reputed to have inquired of another, "I don't think she can be a modest girl to be talked about so much!"

A brilliant lawyer and devastating wit, his talents were given a recognition shared only with AJ Balfour among the Tories – the separate publication of his speeches in Parliament.

During the Covenant Campaign, Smith spoke at five of the demonstrations, coming second only to Carson himself (who spoke at six). The photograph on page 39 catches his typical use of the emphatic physical gesture to reinforce a well-expressed point. In 1919 Smith became Lord Chancellor of England at the age of 46, the youngest holder of that office since the infamous and ferocious Judge Jeffreys.

The Ulster Hall souvenir programme cover (right) was intended not only to be an attractive souvenir for the thousands of Unionists who took part, but also to emphasise that Carson, though pre-eminent in the Campaign, was supported by an array of able men. The Marquess of Londonderry, the Duke of Abercorn and FE Smith played a particularly prominent part in the determined fight to defend the Ulsterman's right to be treated as any other British citizen. In that battle they defended the rights of all, regardless of class or political allegiance.

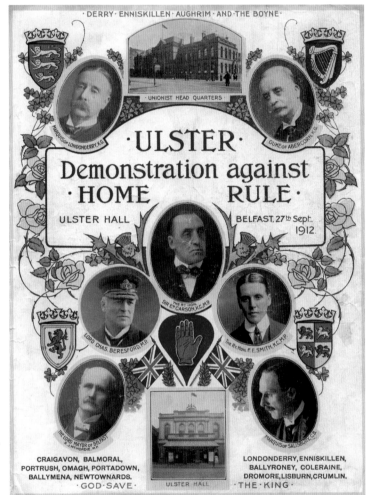

The Ulster Hall Demonstration souvenir programme cover. *(Grand Orange Lodge of Ireland archive)*

ORGANISATION

5

THE SIGNING OF A COVENANT, a solemn and binding declaration of individuals acting as a people, was no light matter. The impressive Covenant Campaign, the prelude to the all-important Covenant Day, was intended to stir the people into action, to explain to them the nature of the commitment they would be asked to make, and to give them the opportunity to hear the leaders whom they were to follow. From the beginning all the organisational ability of a talented people was exploited to the full. As far as possible, nothing would be left to chance; there would be no possibility of misunderstanding the Campaign. All over the Province and beyond, the clear message of Ulster's defiance of a great injustice would be heard.

The words uttered by Unionists were no idle words, but a considered response to the danger which threatened them. No one was left in any doubt of the Unionist leaders' eagerness to make themselves available to the people, to carry throughout Ulster their clear message to stand firm for simple justice and for equal rights.

On 23 September 1912, the Ulster Unionist Council, the elected representative body of Unionism since 1905, met in the Old Town Hall, Belfast, to pass a resolution not only pledging itself to a Covenant but also setting out the case for the action it supported. It proclaimed the supreme right of a people to oppose any law or any government which would deny that people their rights. The Council recognised that, in the time of supreme crisis, "it is needful that we be knit together as one man, each strengthening the other, and not holding back or counting the cost." There spoke that same spirit of independence and self-reliance which had moved Ulster-Scots settlers to join the forces of the American Revolution; for both, liberty was worth any sacrifice.

The photograph on the right on page 42 shows that the solemnity of the occasion was made visually memorable

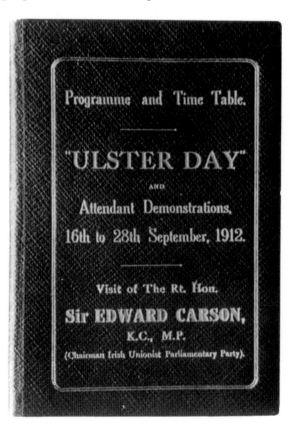

Covenant Campaign and Ulster Day programme and time-table.

ULSTER'S SOLEMN LEAGUE AND COVENANT.

The Resolution.

At the meeting of the Ulster Unionist Council, held on Monday, 23rd September, 1912, the following Resolution was unanimously agreed to, on the proposition of The Marquis of Londonderry, K.G.:—

INASMUCH as we, the duly elected delegates and members of the Ulster Unionist Council, representing all parts of Ulster, are firmly persuaded that by no law can the right to govern those whom we represent be bartered away without their consent; that, although the present Government, the services and sacrifices of our race having been forgotten, may drive us forth from a Constitution which we have ever loyally upheld, they may not deliver us bound into the hands of our enemies; and that it is incompetent for any authority, party, or people to appoint as our rulers a Government dominated by men disloyal to the Empire, and to whom our faith and traditions are hateful;

AND inasmuch as we reverently believe that, as in times past it was given our fathers to save themselves from a like calamity, so now it may be ordered that our deliverance shall be by our own hands; to which end it is needful that we be knit together as one man, each strengthening the other, and none holding back or counting the cost;

THEREFORE we, loyalists of Ulster, ratify and confirm the steps so far taken by the Special Commission this day submitted and explained to us, and we reappoint the Commission to carry on its work on our behalf as in the past;

WE ENTER INTO THE SOLEMN COVENANT appended hereto; and knowing the greatness of the issues depending on our faithfulness, we promise each to the others that, to the uttermost of the strength and means given to us and not regarding any selfish or private interest, our substance and our lives, we will make good the said Covenant;

AND we now bind ourselves in the steadfast determination that, whatever may befall, no such domination shall be thrust upon us, and in the hope that, by the blessing of God, our Union with Great Britain, upon which are fixed our affections and trust, may yet be maintained, and that for ourselves and for our children, for this province and for the whole of Ireland, peace, prosperity, and civil and religious liberty may be secured under the Parliament of the United Kingdom and of the King, whose faithful subjects we are, and will continue all our days.

GOD SAVE THE KING.

The Ulster Unionist Council resolution, 23 September 1912.

The Ulster Unionist Council ratifying the text of the Covenant, 23 September 1912. From *The Graphic*. (PRONI D2638/E/16)

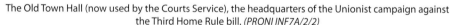

The Old Town Hall (now used by the Courts Service), the headquarters of the Unionist campaign against the Third Home Rule bill. *(PRONI INF7A/2/2)*

Major TVP McCammon, a key figure in organising Ulster Day. *(Grand Orange Lodge of Ireland archive)*

by the display of one of the largest Union Flags ever woven, measuring 48 feet by 25 feet. It was an appropriate gesture, being a reminder to all present that their struggle was a fight to keep the cross of St Patrick in the national flag. It is significant too that the Union Flag is displayed upside down, a distress signal appropriate in a time of crisis.

An Ulster Day Committee had previously been appointed to oversee the whole of the necessary organisation throughout the Province and beyond. The Committee's joint secretaries, Dawson Bates, TVP McCammon and Frank Hall, represented the three powerful and dedicated bodies underpinning the whole effort; the Ulster Unionist Council, the Orange Order and the Unionist Clubs.

The Committee's task of ensuring that all Unionists had the opportunity of signing the Covenant in their own districts was eased by the setting up of local committees responsible for the availability of premises, over 500 of them throughout Ulster, and for all the practical matters

Despatching the Ulster Covenant from the Old Town Hall, 24 September 1912. Volunteers organise the bundles of signature sheets into several hundred cardboard boxes. (PRONI D3275/2)

The marshals at City Hall, Ulster Day, 28 September 1912. They all wore red, white and blue striped armbands bearing the words 'City Hall Guard'. *(PRONI INF7A/2/32)*

which would ensure success. The role of local committees in the districts was vital if the signing of the Covenant was to prove a resounding success.

On 25 September, 700 large cardboard boxes containing copies of the Covenant and the Declaration printed on cardboard in large bold type for display in halls, and forms for signing, were dispatched from the Old Town Hall for distribution throughout Belfast and the rest of Ulster.

In Belfast, where the largest numbers would turn out, careful planning and direction was vital. The Ulster Day organisers were well aware of the danger in bringing together tens of thousands of enthusiastic people; an ill-considered rush could cause serious injuries. Some 2,500 marshals ensured order as the mass of people streamed through the City Hall, each an individual proud to have participated in making a solemn pledge to defend their collective rights.

The marshals set the standard for all with their neat suits and bowler hats. Drawn from the Orange Lodges and the Unionist Clubs, many wore Club badges in their lapels; but they derived their visible authority from their long batons and the special arm bands.

THE DOCUMENT

THE PRESBYTERIANS, WITH THEIR TRADITION of sturdy independence, the very backbone of Ulster Unionism, were well acquainted with the concept of the solemn covenant in the religious history of Scotland in the sixteenth and seventeenth centuries. The Ulster Covenant drew inspiration from the covenants of sixteenth and seventeenth century Scotland, in particular the Scottish National Covenant of 1638 and the Solemn League and Covenant of 1643.

The former was framed in response to Charles I's attempt to impose the new Prayer Book on Scotland, which prompted a riot in St Giles's Cathedral in 1637. In February 1638 the vast majority of Scottish nobles, lairds, ministers and others signed the National Covenant pledging to "maintain the true worship of God" and the "true religion, liberties and laws of the kingdom", and to disobey any orders which contravened them. Although the Scots professed loyalty to Charles I, when confronted with a choice between "true religion" and loyalty to Charles, the former would prevail over the latter.

The covenant of 1643 was issued in the name of the nobility, gentry and ministers of England, Scotland and Ireland and pledged to "bring the Churches of God in the three kingdoms to the nearest conjunction and uniformity in religion." Thus, it may be considered as a British document rather than a purely Scottish one. In retrospect, it was an imperfect understanding between the Scots and the English Parliamentarians. The Scots viewed the Solemn League and Covenant in primarily religious terms but for the English its purpose was primarily political. The Scots wished to preserve and advance the Reformation "according to the Word of God" in the three kingdoms of the British monarchy, whereas the English wished to enlist Scottish military support to defeat Charles I and to secure the rights and liberties of the English and Scottish parliaments. The Scots understood the Reformation "according to the Word of God" to mean the establishment of Presbyterianism in all three kingdoms. When, after the defeat of Charles I, the English parliament, which would not countenance uniformity on the Scottish model, opted for Independency rather than Presbyterianism, the Scots understandably felt betrayed.

What appealed to Ulster unionists was neither the content of these covenants nor the precise historical context but the concept. That Ulster Unionists should draw inspiration from events in sixteenth and seventeenth century Scotland should not be surprising. Ulster is separated from Scotland by the North Channel which is at one point only thirteen miles wide. Historically, this channel has been a link rather than a barrier, and from the earliest times it has witnessed a constant traffic of peoples and ideas between the two coasts. Ulster and Scotland share a strong common Presbyterian heritage. Signatures were collected in Ulster for the Solemn League and Covenant in the 1640s. In the second half of the seventeenth century, people of a Covenanting background, especially from the south-west of Scotland fled government persecution to the milder conditions in Ulster. Men like Thomas Sinclair, the

ULSTER'S
SOLEMN LEAGUE AND COVENANT.

BEING convinced in our consciences that Home Rule would be disastrous to the material well-being of Ulster as well as of the whole of Ireland, subversive of our civil and religious freedom, destructive of our citizenship and perilous to the unity of the Empire, We, whose names are underwritten, MEN of Ulster, loyal subjects of His Gracious Majesty King George V., humbly relying on the God whom our fathers in days of stress and trial confidently trusted, do hereby pledge ourselves in solemn Covenant throughout this our time of threatened calamity to stand by one another in defending for ourselves and our children our cherished position of equal citizenship in the United Kingdom, and in using all means which may be found necessary to defeat the present conspiracy to set up a Home Rule Parliament in Ireland. And, in the event of such a Parliament being forced upon us we further solemnly and mutually pledge ourselves to refuse to recognise its authority. In sure confidence that God will defend the right, We hereto subscribe our names. And further, we individually declare that we have not already signed this Covenant.

Published by the Ulster Day Committee, Unionist Headquarters,
and printed by Henderson & Company. 55, 57 & 59 Donegall St., Belfast.

Placard reproducing the text of the Covenant. *(PRONI D239/004)*

(MEN)   SHEET No _____

PARLIAMENTARY DIVISION, BELFAST
DISTRICT,
PLACE OF SIGNING, CITY HALL.

Covenant :—

BEING CONVINCED in our consciences that Home Rule would be disastrous to the material well-being of Ulster as well as of the whole of Ireland, subversive of our civil and religious freedom, destructive of our citizenship, and perilous to the unity of the Empire, we, whose names are underwritten, men of Ulster, loyal subjects of His Gracious Majesty King George V., humbly relying on the God whom our fathers in days of stress and trial confidently trusted, do hereby pledge ourselves in solemn Covenant, throughout this our time of threatened calamity, to stand by one another in defending, for ourselves and our children, our cherished position of equal citizenship in the United Kingdom, and in using all means which may be found necessary to defeat the present conspiracy to set up a Home Rule Parliament in Ireland. And in the event of such a Parliament being forced upon us, we further solemnly and mutually pledge ourselves to refuse to recognise its authority. In sure confidence that God will defend the right, we hereto subscribe our names.

And further, we individually declare that we have not already signed this Covenant.

NAME.	ADDRESS.

An unused Covenant signature sheet. *(PRONI D239/003)*

(WOMEN)

PARLIAMENTARY DIVISION _____

DISTRICT _____

PLACE OF SIGNING _____

𝔇eclaration :—

We, whose names are underwritten, women of Ulster, and loyal subjects of our gracious King, being firmly persuaded that Home Rule would be disastrous to our Country, desire to associate ourselves with the men of Ulster in their uncompromising opposition to the Home Rule Bill now before Parliament, whereby it is proposed to drive Ulster out of her cherished place in the constitution of the United Kingdom, and to place her under the domination and control of a Parliament in Ireland.

Praying that from this calamity God will save Ireland, we hereto subscribe our names.

NAME.	ADDRESS.

An unused Declaration sheet.

author of the Ulster Covenant, and BDW Montgomery, the Belfast businessman and Secretary of the Ulster Club in Belfast, who suggested the Covenant format, would have had an acute appreciation of this shared heritage.

While the concept came from that tradition, the content of the Ulster Covenant owed much to more recent events. Embedded in its phrases were the democratic ideas of Lord Randolph Churchill who, in 1886, declared that "Ulster will fight and Ulster will be right" and of the Marquess of Salisbury, that Titan among Tory Prime Ministers, who proclaimed that "Parliament has a right to govern the people of Ulster, it has not a right to sell them into slavery."

The Covenant text was the inspired creation of one man, Thomas Sinclair, a wealthy Belfast merchant, a convinced Presbyterian, a son of the twin traditions of the 'Glorious Revolution' of 1688 and the American Revolution of 1776, with their emphasis on human rights and ultimate freedom of action. Sinclair, a modest figure, has long been forgotten, but it was his finely constructed phrases which, in 1912, articulated eternal essential freedoms and thus gave him some claim to be modern Ulster's Thomas Jefferson.

Sinclair's text succinctly presented the Ulster unionist case against the Third Home Rule bill in four key phrases. First, unionists believed that Home Rule would be "disastrous to the material well-being of Ulster as well as the whole of Ireland." Secondly, unionists contended that Home Rule would be "subversive of our civil and religious freedom." Thirdly, unionists were convinced that Home Rule would be "destructive of our citizenship" and "our cherished position of equal citizenship in the United Kingdom." Finally, unionists claimed Home Rule would be "perilous to the unity of the Empire." These four

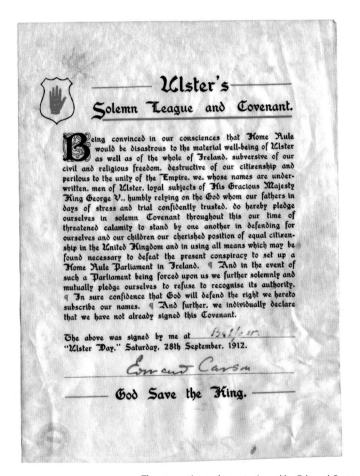

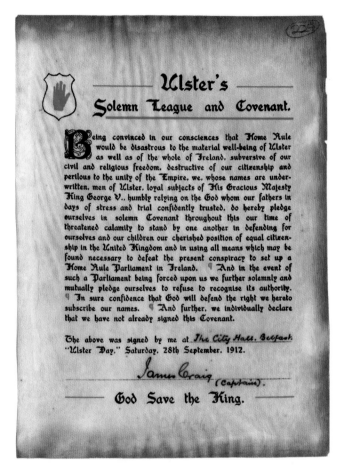

The souvenir parchments signed by Edward Carson and James Craig. *(PRONI D1496/3 & D1413/109)*

propositions encapsulate what might be conveniently described as the economic, the religious, the political and the imperial arguments.

No one can read Sinclair's text, the text of Ulster's Solemn League and Covenant, without being struck by its masterly construction; concise in its wording, comprehensive in its scope and reasonable in its tone, yet conveying a sense of cool determination. It was a document which, given its content and tone, could be signed by a wide range of people with a clear conscience.

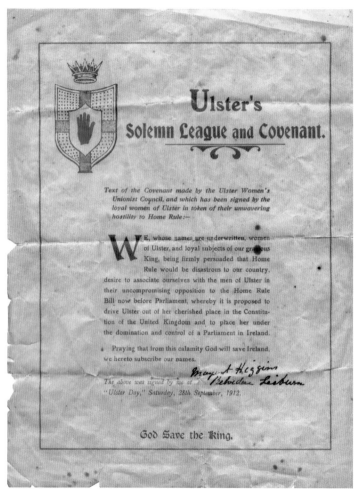

A souvenir Declaration *(Grand Orange Lodge of Ireland archive)*

It was central to the whole purpose of the Covenant that it should be regarded as binding by every individual who signed it. The Unionist leaders, calling on the people to prepare themselves for possibly unparalleled sacrifices, ensured that they knew what they were defending and to what they committed themselves. Before signing every person was given the opportunity to read the prominently-placed placards bearing the Covenant text, which decorated all the signing centres.

The Ulster Day Committee dispatched to every local committee supplies of the blank Covenant sheets. Each sheet carried the full text of the Covenant and allowed 10 men to sign and give their addresses.

Local committees were supplied by the Ulster Day Committee with quantities of the parallel women's Declaration, a document which allowed the women "to associate with the men of Ulster in their uncompromising opposition to the Home Rule Bill now before Parliament." Each sheet could also take 10 names and addresses.

The 218,206 men who signed the Covenant in Ulster were offered a souvenir of their commitment, a copy on parchment paper of the famous text. In many Ulster homes these souvenirs occupied pride of place and very many have survived as a lasting memorial to the tens of thousands of Ulstermen who were determined to face a great crisis.

The 228,991 women who signed the parallel Declaration in Ulster were offered their own souvenir copy on parchment paper. Asked to make no less a sacrifice than their men folk and motivated by the same ideals, these women are also remembered along with the men with whom they associated themselves.

7

WOMEN

MEN PROVIDED THE LEADERSHIP OF Unionism but they were men who, knowing the strengths of women, wished to give women the vote. Indeed, the Ulster Crisis was to allow a noticeable shift in the role of women and secured for them a relatively advanced position. An Ulster Women's Unionist Council had been formed in 1911, and

Miss Whitaker, Honorary Secretary of West Belfast Ulster Women's Unionist Association canvassing. *(PRONI INF7A/2/20)*

within a year of its formation, the UWUC had become the largest female political organisation in the history of Ireland, with an estimated membership of between 40,000 and 50,000. During the first month of the organisation's existence, more than 4,000 women joined the West Belfast Association alone.

The Covenant Campaign, with its emphasis on the unity of all Loyalists, harnessed the vital contribution of women, recognising their particular concern to secure the future and the rightful inheritance of Ulster's children.

The conventions of the time might demand a separate women's Declaration, but women were eager to show that they could not only match but outstrip the efforts of the men. Everywhere they helped in the tremendous efforts to organise the gathering of signatures. Well aware of the often unrelenting demands of domestic life, Unionist women went from door to door canvassing the support of their fellow women. The efforts of these dedicated workers for Ulster's future paid off handsomely. In Ulster 218,206 men signed the Covenant; the women, reflecting their numerical superiority in the population, beat that with a figure of 228,991.

Two of the most impressive features of the Covenant Campaign, were the breadth of Unionist support across the classes and the high profile of women.

The photograph on page 51 shows Miss Whitaker, honorary secretary of West Belfast Ulster Women's Unionist Association, canvassing women in a poor district of the constituency. Women were asked to sign the parallel Declaration associating them with the men "in their uncompromising opposition to the Home Rule Bill now before Parliament." In truth canvassing was unnecessary; men and women of all classes needed little prompting to sign the Covenant and the Declaration respectively.

The Women's Unionist Association in the East Antrim constituency produced a poster to advertise the local efforts to publicise the Declaration. Women were exhorted to bring their older children to one of the religious services and then to sign the Declaration.

Throughout Ulster women, rich and poor alike, streamed into the halls made available for the signing of the women's Declaration. Working class women seldom had any alternative but to bring their children along with them as can be seen in the photograph on page 52. Though they may not have understood the seriousness of the occasion, the young off-spring were thus made witnesses to a great moment in Ulster's history – a moment in which their mothers played a full part.

8

RELIGION

AT THE ROOT OF ULSTER's protest lay a sense of immediate danger, immediate danger to the traditional freedom of conscience enjoyed by Protestants and central to their way of life and thinking. That was the gap in Ireland; the unbridgeable gap between Dublin and Belfast; the unbridgeable gap between different understandings of religious authority, citizenship and political identity/destiny.

Ulster Day was a day for reflection and prayer. There was nothing of vacuous outward show; every gesture and action sprang from the deepest convictions of a sturdily independent people who desired peace, who longed only for the right to live their lives after their own fashion.

All over Ulster some 500 religious services were held on the morning of Ulster Day, bringing together representatives of all the Protestant denominations.

Many of the services thundered forth what was already almost Ulster's national anthem, "O God Our Help in Ages Past," amid a rich mixture of emotions; faith in God, faith in the justice of their cause, faith in their shared experiences as a people and faith in one another.

Commentators found everywhere an atmosphere charged with religious devotion. The London *Daily Telegraph* observed:

> "The more strictly political objects of the Covenant derive all their strength and stability from this religious character."

The *Belfast News Letter* noted that "religion lies at the very foundation of the lives of the people." Of Ulster Day

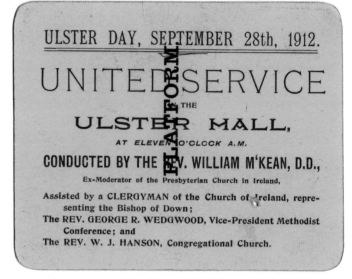

An invitation to the Ulster Day special religious service held at the Ulster Hall. *(PRONI D1422/B/13/32)*

itself the same newspaper declared: "This was no occasion for demonstration, but for dedication to a high purpose."

The religious dimension was reinforced by the display of support for the people's actions on the part of the Protestant Churches. Charles Frederick D'Arcy, then Bishop of Down and Connor and Dromore, and later Archbishop of Armagh, summed up the position when he declared:

> "we hold that no power, not even the British Parliament, has the right to deprive us of our heritage of British citizenship."

The Marshals' religious service in the courtyard of the City Hall, Ulster Day. *(PRONI INF7A/2/31)*

Before the signing of the Covenant started in Belfast, a religious service was held in the Ulster Hall with representatives of the Presbyterian, Anglican, Methodist and Congregational Churches all participating. This and all the other services throughout Ulster reminded everyone present of the solemnity of their individual commitment in signing the Covenant.

Of the 2,500 marshals appointed to keep order at or near the City Hall on Ulster Day many met first for a special religious service in the courtyard of the City Hall as shown in the photograph above. Having dedicated their efforts to God, they marched out to commence their day's work, the onerous but all-important task of ensuring that the signing was effected with maximum efficiency.

In Banbridge, County Down, there were simultaneous religious services in the Parish Church (conducted by the Rev Ussher Greer, the Rector), Scarva Street Presbyterian Church (conducted by the Rev Thomas Boyd and RB Knox), the Methodist Church (conducted by the Rev Sherwood) and the Baptist Church (conducted by Pastors HM Carleton and W Campbell).

In Portadown, County Armagh, the service in the Parish Church was conducted by the Rev Chancellor Hobson, assisted by the Rev HB Cooke; in the Methodist Church by the Rev George R Wedgwood, the Vice-President of the Methodist Conference; in the First Presbyterian Church by the Rev WJ Macaulay, assisted by the Rev AR Fee; and in the Armagh Road Church by the Rev HW Perry. Services were also held in Drumcree Parish Church, Seagoe Parish Church, St Saviour's Parish Church (Dobbin) and Knocknamuckley Parish Church.

In Dungannon, County Tyrone, a service was held in the Parish Church, where the address was given by the Rev TJ McEndoo, the rector, while both Presbyterian churches held a united service in the First Presbyterian Church, at which the Rev Samuel Lindsay preached. The service in the Methodist Church was conducted by the Rev RJ Elliott, and in the Baptist Church by the Rev Thomas Warwick.

A standard service sheet was produced for such gatherings, though the choice of hymns and lessons was a matter for local people.

Many of the hymns and lessons contained words of particular importance to a people under threat. There was an overwhelming sense of dependence on God's protection. Hence the lines: "O Lord, stretch forth Thy mighty hand, And guard and bless our Fatherland."

Ulster Day Special Service sheet. (*Grand Orange Lodge of Ireland archive*)

A PRAYER FOR ULSTER DAY.

I.

O ALMIGHTY GOD who, in the days of our fathers, didst save our country, delivering it from many perils, and didst establish among us peace and security, with the knowledge of Thy truth; look upon us in Thy mercy at this time of great national danger and stretch forth Thine arm to help us. We confess to Thee our many sins, and acknowledge that we are not worthy of all the loving-kindness which Thou hast shown to us. Yet, we pray Thee, turn not away Thy favour from us, and, in Thine infinite mercy, preserve to us and to our children that heritage of truth and of liberty, of peace and of fruitful labour, which Thou hast guarded for us hitherto. Avert the dreadful evils of civil and religious strife which now threaten, and grant to us and to all dwellers in this land the blessings of unity and brotherly concord, that righteousness and happiness may flourish among us to all generations.

II.

G RANT, O LORD, we beseech Thee, to all our leaders in Church and State, and especially to those who are now guiding us through this time of danger and perplexity, the spirit of wisdom and understanding, that they may have a right judgment in all things, and that, setting aside all worldly ambitions, they may seek Thy glory and the welfare of Thy people. Grant to them strength and faithfulness, with stedfastness of heart, that, shunning all rashness, they may be enabled to maintain the right and set forward truth and justice. Direct all their endeavours, and crown them with such success that the unity of our commonwealth may be preserved and that discord may cease among us.

III.

G RANT, O LORD, to the people of our community such patience and self-control that no occasion of bitterness may have power to move them. Restrain all angry passions, and enable us, with unshaken confidence, to commit ourselves unto Thee, and, with constancy and firmness, to maintain the cause for which we stand.

These petitions we present in the name of Jesus Christ, our Lord and Saviour. AMEN.

A Prayer for Ulster Day.

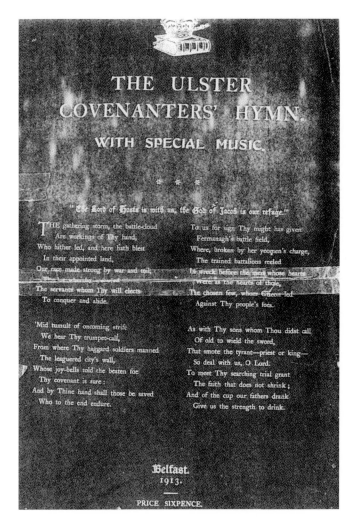

Ulster Covenanters' Hymn, published in 1913.

The specially written prayer for the Ulster Day services was properly humble in tone. Amid the growing crisis, faced by civil war, the upholders of Ulster's rights asked that God might help them as He had helped their forefathers, might bring them peace and assist them to "Restrain all angry passions." For the great players in the political drama (the leaders of the Church and State, and the leaders of the Unionist cause) there was an appeal that God might help them achieve "the spirit of wisdom and understanding."

The moving spectacle of Ulstermen uniting together in one mind and with one purpose before their God inspired the production of many poems, songs and hymns. The Ulster Covenanters' Hymn (page 57), published in 1913, identified Ulster's struggle for survival with the struggle of the ancient Israelites. There is a covenant between God and His people, but it is a covenant which requires that the favoured people keep faith with God: "And of the cup our fathers drank, Give us the strength to drink."

ULSTER DAY IN BELFAST

ULSTER WAS THE ONLY PART of the island to experience the full vigour of the Industrial Revolution and early twentieth century Belfast one of the major industrial powerhouses of the world. The city could boast "the greatest shipyard, rope works, tobacco factory, linen mill, dry dock and tea machinery works in the world".

Saturday was then a normal working day but on Saturday 28 September 1912, "the industrial heart of the great city was still: the great shipyards were silent; the looms were idle in the linen mills; the rope works and foundries were deserted."

The city centre was the focus of attention; understandably so with the presence of Carson and the Unionist leadership, the huge crowds and the magnificent new City Hall as the setting for the proceedings.

After the religious service at the Ulster Hall to prepare themselves solemnly, and to dedicate Ulster unionism's cause in honest religious conscience, the Unionist leaders marched in procession to the City Hall. This imposing building, built between 1896 and 1906 in fine imperial style, with overtones of Indian empire, therefore became the focus of attention for the massive crowds of Unionist men and women who filled the city. The leaders arrived at the City Hall shortly after noon, accompanied by a guard of honour headed by the Boyne Standard, which swirled proudly in the early autumn breeze. Carson, Charles Beresford (top hat), and FE Smith (bowler) and Craig are clearly seen in the photograph opposite as they pass along Bedford Street coming from the Ulster Hall. It is worth noting how Lord Carson is being acclaimed by women as he advances through the crowds behind the marshals.

The march of the leaders from the Ulster Hall was carefully planned and helped increase the public spectacle of the day. To have held the religious service and the signing ceremony in the one building would have weakened the impact on the Ulster public, and on the multitude of pressmen who reported the proceedings of Ulster Day to the world.

The leaders march to Belfast City Hall after the religious service in the Ulster Hall.
(PRONI INF7A/2/34)

Carson signs the Covenant. *(PRONI INF7A/2/49)*

Carson was the first of the leaders to sign the Covenant; he was after all referred to by the senior men of Unionism as 'The Chief'. Around him in the photograph opposite stand a host of other Unionist dignitaries. Interestingly Craig, the organisational genius behind the faultless planning of Ulster Day, did not sign the Covenant Declaration immediately after Carson. Craig was not possessed of a centre-stage ego. Making things happen was more important to him than the limelight. He realised that Carson, with his immense parliamentary presence and national status, had to be the unrivalled public leader of Unionism in its hour of crisis. Therefore, after Carson had signed with the specially made silver pen presented to him for the occasion, Craig gave precedence, as can be seen from the photograph of the leaders' Covenant Declaration form (page 36), to Lord Londonderry, the leaders of the main Protestant Churches, and then to other lesser men than himself, in the order of signing. The *Northern Whig* commented on the calibre of the Unionist elite who signed the Covenant with Carson in the great marble vestibule of the City Hall:

> "By 12.15 there was gathered round the flag-covered drumhead [the round table covered with the Union Flag] a body of men who represented a very large part of the capital, the talent, the genius, and the energy of the City of Belfast. If the Covenant is treason, nearly all that makes for progress in this city will have to be impeached."

There were many other signing centres in Belfast but more people signed the Covenant at the City Hall than at any of the 500 venues across Ulster; 35,000 men in all.

Practical organisation was the very foundation of Ulster Day. Before the crowds could be let into the Belfast City Hall carpenters had to fit out the corridors with temporary desks.

The still scene shown in the photograph below would be quickly ended when thousands streamed into the City Hall to sign the Covenant, as depicted in *The Graphic* on page 62. The marshals ensured that the signatories were directed to the desks as quickly as possible and moved away with equal speed in order to let others take their places.

The temporary desks and neatly arranged signature sheets wait inside the City Hall in anticipation of the crowds of Ulster Day. *(PRONI INF7A/2/46)*

"WE WILL NOT HAVE HOME RULE": THE CHIEF ACT OF THE REMARKABLE ULSTER DAY DEMONSTRATIONS IN BELFAST.

DRAWN BY S. BEGG, OUR SPECIAL ARTIST IN BELFAST.

(Belfast Central Library Newspaper Archive)

Crowd scene in Belfast on Ulster Day, looking east towards Chichester Street and Donegall Square East. *(PRONI INF7A/2/40)*

This photograph, taken at 2.05 pm according to the clock on the Robinson and Cleaver Building, shows a crowd, slightly reduced from that gathered at noon for the arrival of Carson and the other Unionist leaders at the City Hall. The reason may have been that after the excitement of the leadership procession and Carson's signing of the Covenant Declaration, which symbolised Ulster's regretful determination to resist Westminster's Home Rule tyranny, the initial crowds thinned for lunch.

The view above was produced by joining two photographs together and it provides irrefutable evidence of the vast crowd that thronged Belfast city centre on Ulster Day. As such it is comparable to the wide-angle crowd photographs taken from Belfast City Hall, which were published by the Belfast paper the *News Letter* after the Unionist demonstrations of November 1985 and November 1986 against the Anglo-Irish Agreement signed at Hillsborough by Mrs Thatcher and Dr Garret Fitzgerald on 15 November

Panoramic view of the Ulster Day crowd in Belfast, looking south across Donegall Square, probably from the Robinson and Cleaver Building, with the east side of the Square on the immediate left of centre and its west side on the far right. *(PRONI INF7A/2/37)*

1985. With the Ulster Day scenes of the Carson era deeply embedded in the cultural memory of the Unionist community it was inevitable that the children, grandchildren and great grandchildren of men and women who stood before Belfast City Hall on 28 September 1912, should have returned there, to register their protest at what they then perceived to be the most recent attempt to deny them their birthright as full British citizens.

This photograph, timed at 3.20 pm by the clock on the Robinson and Cleaver Building, shows the tightly packed crowds that surrounded the Belfast City Hall for most of Ulster Day. *(PRONI INF7A/2/41)*

Ulster Day
crowd scene
looking down
Donegall
Place towards
Royal Avenue.
*(Grand Orange
Lodge of Ireland
archive)*

The crowds were impressively dense again shortly after 3.00 pm, as is evidenced by the photograph opposite.

The photograph above is probably the most iconic one of the Ulster Day crowd in Belfast. It shows the magnitude of the crowd which not only packs Donegall Place but also stretches, as far as the eye can see, to Royal Avenue and beyond. Appropriately, the photograph has the statue of the Queen-Empress Victoria dominating the scene, a figure who, during her long reign, came to symbolise that Kingdom and Empire of which Ulster Unionists passionately desired to remain a part.

ULSTER—*THE HAND AND THE MAN: SIR EDWARD CARSON SIGNING THE COVENANT IN THE CITY HALL*

The drawing above accurately conveys the dignity which attended Carson's signing of the Covenant. However, as a drawing it obviously reflects the impressions the artist had of the scene he was portraying. In this respect it differs from the precise photographic image on page 60 but allied to the accompanying *Graphic* caption and the heading "THE HAND AND THE MAN", it clearly makes the point, more so than the photograph, that at the moment of signing, Carson represented Ulster and Ulster knew it could have no better champion.

Ulster Day in Belfast was remarkable for the orderly deportment of the crowds of ordinary Unionist people who resolutely gathered in the city to record their opposition to the Government's Irish policy, and to prove that the Duke of Abercorn's declaration at the time of the Second Home Rule Bill in 1892, "We will not have Home Rule", which had been shortened by general Ulster usage to "We will not have it", held good in 1912 when the third attempt to place Ulster under a Dublin Parliament was being made. The only time when the good order of the day's proceedings was threatened, was when the initial rush of the crowd of men waiting to sign the Covenant declarations surged into the City Hall. This was understandable. The crowd was so vast that the pressure at the entry gates must have been like the wave of humanity, only multiplied tenfold, that assails the Windsor Park turnstiles when Northern Ireland is playing a crucial World Cup decider. What red-blooded Ulsterman would not have wanted to be able to tell his children, in future years, that, after Carson and the other Unionist leaders, he had been first to sign the Covenant? Again the artist of *The Graphic* captured well, and sympathetically, not only the scene but the feelings of the unionist people for its British readership.

On the evening of Ulster Day Carson dined in the Ulster Club, an elegant Regency-style building at Castle Junction, with Robert James McMordie, the Lord Mayor of Belfast. He delivered a speech from the upper windows of this building to the assembled crowds below, "solid masses of people tens of thousands in number", who escorted him to the docks to the Liverpool boat. Carson had been in Ulster for nearly a fortnight prior to the signing of the Covenant, fulfilling his role as leader of the anti-Home Rule movement. Now he was

THE RUSH TO SIGN THE COVENANT
THE CROWD STORMING THE GATES OF THE CITY HALL

"To stem the impetuous, incessant torrent that poured through, [the gates] had to be kept partially closed and held fast by batons thrust in as wedges." *The Graphic* (Belfast Central Library Newspaper Archive)

The scene outside the Ulster Club, Castle Junction, Belfast, on the evening of Ulster Day. (PRONI D961/3/003)

The SS *Patriotic*, the ship in which Carson sailed to Liverpool.
(Grand Orange Lodge of Ireland archive)

preparing to take the fight to England where the politics of empire were decided. The docks were only a few minutes' walk away but it took an hour for Carson's wagonette, drawn not by horses but by men, to reach its destination.

Carson took the steamship, the appropriately named SS *Patriotic*, to Liverpool at 21:15. The shipyard workers of the Queen's Island Unionist Club provided a guard of honour around the shed of the Belfast Steam Ship Company. From the upper deck of the SS *Patriotic*, Carson enjoined the huge crowd of loyal well-wishers on the dockside, to hold to their Covenant pledge made that day, and concluded with the defiant battlecry of the unconquered heroes of Londonderry in 1689: "Keep the old flag flying and No Surrender!"

In June 1690 bonfires greeted the arrival of King William III in Ulster. On Ulster Day a huge bonfire on the historic Cave Hill, and other smaller bonfires on either side of Belfast Lough, marked Carson's departure. These events are the subject of 'A Question of Covenants', a more recent

AFTER THE COVENANT: THE LEADER'S FAREWELL
"I ASK YOU TO KEEP THE FLAG FLYING — NO SURRENDER!"

An artist's impression of Carson's leave-taking. *(Belfast Central Library Newspaper Archive)*

poem by the Belfast-born but Dublin-based poet Gerald Dawe.

The next day, Sunday 29 September 1912, Carson addressed a very large crowd of pro-Union supporters, estimated at 150,000 strong, almost immediately upon his disembarkation at Merseyside. The Liverpool crowd, many of whom were of Ulster unionist origins, sang the Unionist battle-hymn 'O God, our Help in Ages Past'. By turning up on a chilly dockside at 7.30 am, they showed that they were solidly behind their kith and kin and fellow citizens in Ulster. That evening further evidence of their solidarity was provided when Carson addressed another rally in Liverpool.

The Graphic published an artist's impression of the ordinary Unionists who were called upon to sign the Covenant. The sketches convey a simple fact, namely that the mass of Unionists who poured into Belfast and into other centres on Ulster Day were not men who enjoyed any privilege, other than the privilege open to all; citizenship of a great democracy with a powerful empire. To even ordinary Unionists, their position within the United Kingdom was their supreme inheritance; all else paled into insignificance.

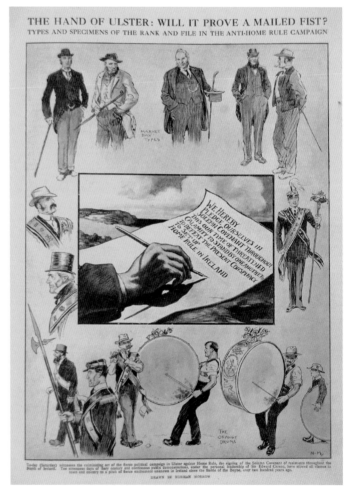

'Rank and file unionists', *The Graphic*, 28 September 1912. *(Belfast Central Library Newspaper Archive)*

10

ULSTER DAY: OUTSIDE BELFAST

The vast crowds gathered in Belfast, the capital of Ulster, were impressive and caught the imagination of much of the Press. However, without the rest of Ulster the Covenant would not have been a success. It was a fact recognised by the Ulster Day Committee when it dispatched 700 boxes of forms for signature to the many local committees.

In villages and towns all over Ulster, Unionists shut up their shops and their homes, and walked or took a car to the nearest centre to sign the Covenant. The sense of special occasion was overwhelming; streets bedecked with flags and bunting, cars displaying Union Flags and unionists dressed in their best clothes, wearing loyal badges. Though it was the height of the harvest in the countryside, the farmers laid down their scythes and, in many cases, trudged miles to share in the privilege of signing. Unionists, urban and rural, rich and poor, peer and pauper, farmer and factory worker, were all fired by the same vision of unbreakable unity in adversity.

For example, in Omagh, Co Tyrone, it was reported that:

"The signatures to the Covenant included all the Protestant clergymen of the district, the professional gentlemen, business men, magistrates and all those of affluence and position, while the Protestant tradesmen and artisans may be said to have signed it to a man. The list of signatures was much more extensive than was anticipated and the large number of parchment certificates which had been issued was found to be insufficient."

Ulster Day in Enniskillen. *(Grand Orange Lodge of Ireland archive)*

All over the Province the determination of Belfast's Unionists was matched, even outstripped. In the Nationalist-dominated areas of rural Ulster, Unionists were not discouraged but perhaps were even more determined to participate in Ulster Day. There were some nasty incidents, such as the attack on a Unionist farmer and his family, including children, in County Monaghan.

threatened and betrayed by the prospect of a Dublin dominated Home Rule parliament. Nevertheless, they played their full part in Ulster Day, aware of its especial importance to them. In County Donegal almost 18,000 people signed either the Covenant or Declaration. In Monaghan almost 10,500 people signed and in Cavan the two documents attracted just over 8,000 signatories. In the photograph to the left the men of Raphoe, County Donegal, are turned out to sign the Covenant.

The women of Raphoe were as well acquainted with the consequences of Home Rule as the men folk and turned out with equal determination. In the photograph below the women sign the parallel Declaration.

Men signing the Covenant on Ulster Day at Raphoe. *(PRONI D1422/B/13/32)*

However, the outrages were doubtless seen as merely a test of the even greater resolve which would be necessary in the seemingly dark days ahead.

After a service in Enniskillen Parish Church, where the Bishop of Clogher emphasised the religious aspect of the occasion to a congregation of 2,000, the would-be signatories marched to the Town Hall, accompanied by local yeomanry. The first to sign was the Earl of Erne, His Majesty's Lieutenant for Fermanagh. The second name was that of Dr Maurice Day, the Bishop of Clogher.

The unionists of Cavan, Donegal and Monaghan, heavily outnumbered by the nationalists, felt particularly

Women signing the Declaration on Ulster Day at Raphoe. *(PRONI D1422/B/13/32)*

ULSTER DAY: OUTSIDE ULSTER

11

WHILE THE FATE OF ULSTER clearly lay in the hands of its population, some effort was made to accommodate Ulster folk no longer resident in their native land but eager to identify themselves with the great struggle which loomed ahead. Outside of Ulster, if men and women could provide proof of their place of birth, they were allowed to associate themselves with the Covenant. Signatures came from Dublin (2,000 men signed there) and from all over Great Britain; Edinburgh, Glasgow, York, Liverpool, London, Manchester and Bristol. In all 24,217 'expatriates' signed; 19,162 men and 5,055 women.

Such was the enthusiasm of unionist folk absent from their native land that they determined to identify with their province in its time of crisis. Not even the Atlantic could form a barrier. A letter from a passenger on the SS *Lake Champlain* bound for Montreal, Canada, from Liverpool, explained how Ulster Day was celebrated aboard that ship and remarked on the puzzlement felt by the English. Attached to the letter were the signatures of 12 second-class passengers, four men and eight women.

The third-class passengers on the SS *Lake Champlain* also got hold of the text of the

A letter written on board the SS *Lake Champlain* containing the signatures of 12 passengers. (PRONI D1327/3/96)

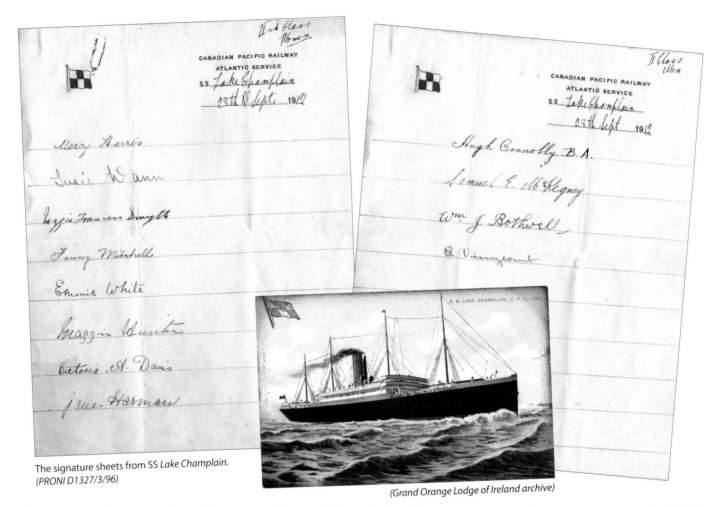

The signature sheets from SS *Lake Champlain*.
(PRONI D1327/3/96)

(Grand Orange Lodge of Ireland archive)

Covenant, stuck it on a piece of paper and signed their names on the document thus created. In all there were 34 passengers in this class of Ulster extraction.

In Nanking, China, nine men signed the Covenant, eight of whom were sailors serving aboard HMS *Monmouth*. Fifty-six men signed the Covenant in Winnipeg and Alberta, Canada; 39 men in Perth, Western Australia; and 23 men in the United States.

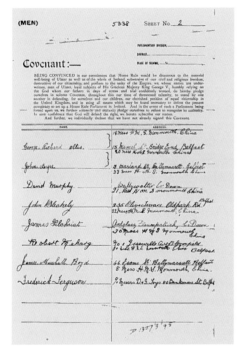

Signatories in Nanking, China, including those serving on HMS *Monmouth*. *(PRONI D1327/3/95)*

The signing of the Ulster Covenant in Manchester. *(Grand Orange Lodge of Ireland archive)*

In Manchester 458 people signed the Ulster Covenant and Women's Declaration: 353 men and 105 women. Among these signatories to the Covenant were Alderman Jason Thompson, the Manchester Provincial Grand Treasurer, who had been born in Enniskillen, and who was a member of Earl of Enniskillen LOL 557, an Oldham lodge; James Jackson, District Master of Manchester District who lived at 57 Albert Street, Bradford, Manchester, a member of Affability LOL 256 and had been born in Clones, County Monaghan; and the District Treasurer, Richard Quinton who had been born in Enniskillen and was a member of Earl of Roden LOL 184.

The District Master of Oldham District, George Keast, who had been born in Newry; the district chaplain, Edward Brooks, born in Armagh; the district treasurer John Bladd, born in County Fermanagh; James Wardle the master of LOL 11, who had been born in Belfast; and Charles H Ashton, the secretary of LOL 564, who had also been born in Belfast, also signed the Covenant in Manchester.

12

THE PRESS

WITH FEW EXCEPTIONS, THE ULSTER and British press declared Ulster Day to have been successful as a massive display of Unionist resolve to oppose the Third Home Rule Bill. Even papers favourable to the Liberal Government could not deny the significance of the Ulster Day Demonstration in Belfast, nor fail to recognise that the Unionists were clearly not, as they had often been portrayed, bluffing in their preparations for resisting the imposition of Dublin rule. The *London Star* was one such Liberal paper that, grudgingly perhaps, faced up to the reality that the opponents of Unionism had to accept that the Ulstermen meant business. It considered it "folly to belittle or to deride the Ulster Covenant." Avoiding the natural Liberal "temptation", which was "great", to "assail these Covenanters with mockery", the *Star* stated that it "instinctively" shrank "from treating with levity the disciplined vow taken by these Ulster Protestants. It is not a thing to be laughed at. It is a thing to be reckoned with."

There was an acknowledgement of reality in this assessment that was singularly lacking from the report of the Belfast Nationalist newspaper the *Irish News,* which alone found it possible to dismiss the protest:

> "Taking the day's proceedings altogether they were tame as a demonstration of enthusiasm, and highly ludicrous as an indication of the 'grim determined spirit.' The whole grotesque production has been a political failure, though a comic success. ... A covenant has been signed by great numbers of people – many of whom had never read its terms."

The pro-Unionist, Belfast-published newspapers, the *News Letter* and the *Northern Whig,* could be expected to give a favourable report of the happenings of Ulster Day, but even they seemed taken aback by the overwhelming way the Unionist people had responded to the calls from their leaders to support the Covenant, and show the world their mettle. The *Northern Whig* noted that all classes of Unionists had signed the Covenant with "not a man of them who did not know what the celebration meant." It then indulged in some purple prose, which it was entitled to do given the achievement of the Unionist people on Ulster Day, when it parodied Macaulay's *Lays of Ancient Rome* by continuing that no one signed "who did not feel that in these ceremonies he was paying a duty to the ashes of his fathers and the temple of his God." Ulster Day had given fitting prominence to the Union Jack, "the glorious old flag, emblem of the unity of Britain, which met the gaze at every footstep." The *News Letter* referred to the "wonderful sense of order" that had marked the behaviour of the crowds with an "ever present … sense of individual responsibility underlying the business of the day."

The London *Daily Express* clearly understood the true significance of the Ulster people's exhibition of solidarity on Ulster Day:

> "Even the most obtuse and the least sincere can no longer pretend to misunderstand the mood of Ulster. The deeply impressive scenes and ceremonies of Covenant Day throughout the province were the culmination of a campaign of preparation conceived and executed in

SIR E. CARSON IN LIVERPOOL.

GREAT ENTHUSIASM.

(FROM OUR SPECIAL CORRESPONDENT.)

LIVERPOOL, SUNDAY.

The Patriotic reached Liverpool at half-past seven this morning. As she approached the Princes' landing stage a roar of cheering arose from a vast multitude, comprising many thousands of people. The scene was a remarkable one. The landing stage itself was closely packed for at least half its length; another crowd, just as large, occupied the roofing of sheds, while, beyond and above them, there was a third tier of densely congregated people lining the road. The enormous assemblage at that hour on a Sunday morning was a surprise to everyone, and the unrestrained enthusiasm was such as could not have been anticipated in an English city. Hats and handkerchiefs were waved, and the cheering maintained uninterruptedly. It gained strength, too, in deep outbursts as Sir Edward Carson, Mr. F. E. Smith, Lord Charles Beresford, and Lord Londonderry appeared at the rails, and acknowledged the welcome. As the vessel drew alongside a brass band played the Ulster Anthem, "O, God, our help in ages past."

Orange sashes were prominently worn by a great many persons in the crowd, and two Lodge banners were carried aloft.

Sir Edward Carson and Mr. Smith were the first to land. Amidst continued cheering, they were greeted by Alderman Salvidge, J.P., Chairman of the Liverpool Conservative Workingmen's Association.

ADDRESS TO SIR E. CARSON.

When the resounding vocal demonstration subsided, at the bidding of the leaders. Alderman Salvidge read and presented to Sir Edward Carson an address on behalf of the Conservative workingmen of Liverpool. The address was in the following terms:—

We, representing the Unionist workingmen of Liverpool and district, give you a hearty welcome to this city. We gratefully acknowledge your magnificent efforts to preserve the integrity of the Empire, and to save from the tyranny of a Nationalist Parliament in Dublin our fellow loyalists in Ireland.

We are proud to think that in this time of crisis our Irish compatriots are led by such a commander. Your profound experience of Irish affairs, the tenacity and courage which you displayed in stamping out lawlessness during a memorable period of Irish history, and the self-sacrifice and devotion which you have again and again shown in the cause of Ireland and the unity of the Empire are nowhere more appreciated than in Liverpool.

The series of great demonstrations which have been held in Ulster, the expressed determination of the Loyalists of Ireland not to be driven outside the Imperial bond at the bidding of a Government on whose neck Mr. Redmond's heel has been placed—these have made it clear that Ulster will do its part in overthrowing the Home Rule conspiracy. We, the Unionists of Liverpool, are equally re-

THE ULSTER COVENANT SIGNED.

UNPARALLELED SCENES IN BELFAST.

IRISH UNIONISTS MAKING HISTORY.

EARNEST RELIGIOUS SERVICES.

GREAT ENTHUSIASM OF THE PEOPLE.

REMARKABLE ACHIEVEMENT OF ORGANISATION.

SIR EDWARD CARSON'S RECEPTION AND DEPARTURE.

HIS FINAL DECLARATION—"NO SURRENDER."

CELEBRATIONS THROUGHOUT THE PROVINCE.

UNIONIST LEADERS IN LIVERPOOL.

THE ULSTER CAMPAIGN.

TEN NOTABLE DAYS.

Not for a century at least have the population of Ulster been so deeply roused as they have been during the fortnight which ended with Saturday last—Ulster Day. The heart-stirring of the Ulster Protestants, their profound earnestness, their firm resolve to resist Home Rule if the Radical and Nationalist coalition at Westminster should attempt to force such a measure upon them, has been demonstrated in such a way since the first of a great series of meetings was held at historic Enniskillen on the 18th inst., that the campaign is surely destined to form a land mark in the future history of Ireland and her relations with England.

These Ulster demonstrations were inaugurated at Enniskillen, which may be described as a stronghold of Unionism in the south-western side of the province. Here Sir Edward Carson, under the chairmanship of the Earl of Erne, opened the campaign, and around his platform that day stood thousands of sturdy Fermanagh men, who listened to his advice, and who declared their readiness to resist the imposition of Home Rule upon them by every means in their power. Sir Edward Carson, who has just completed a stressful fortnight in Ulster, then said that the Unionists of the North were laying the foundation for their defence, and that they would enter into the most solemn Covenant, one with another, that in all steps that may be necessary to resist the Home Rule scheme, even though it became law, they would advance as one man. The speaker and his audience seemed to be at one in this declaration. When Sir Edward, in the middle of his speech on Portora hill, repeated the words of Colonel Wolseley, addressed to Enniskillen men previous to the battle of Newtownbutler, and asked the men before him whether they would advance or retire, the multitude, with one voice, defiantly shouted "Advance." One can hardly doubt that these men would follow their leaders with fearless determination to uphold the cause which they believe to be just and right. Lord Hugh Cecil, who was the only Englishman who addressed that meeting, remarked that day they were making history. As to self-government for Ireland, he contended that the Union was not inconsistent with that. It was not for subjection or dependency that they contended, but for the right of united self-government, by a free people for the cause of freedom and order. At the close of the proceedings, in which Mr. Fetherstonhaugh M.P.; Mr. Horner, M.P., and Mr. Thomas Sinclair also took a prominent part, the meeting with one acclaim affirmed the resolve of the great Ulster Convention of 1892—"We will not have Home Rule." This resolution was adopted at the whole series of meetings.

On the following day Sir Edward Carson attended a meeting of the Ulster Unionist Council in Belfast, and on that day the terms of the Covenant, which was so extensively signed on Saturday last, were agreed to and published. It was on the same day that the declaration of the Unionist women of Ulster was formulated and given to the public. In the evening the Irish Unionist leader proceeded to Lisburn, where he had a reception not less warm and hearty than the one

The *Irish Times* of 30 September 1912. (PRONI INF7A/2/52)

the obvious spirit of religious and patriotic fervour. You may call that fanaticism if you will. [The *Express* did not.] To call it bluff, or to deny the desperate earnestness which inspires it is quite impossible. Ulster will not have Home Rule, and all the world now knows it."

The London *Times*, which in those days was sympathetic to the Unionist cause, caught the mood and deeper meaning of the Covenant campaign. Its assessment was above all based on political reality:

"English readers have followed in detail and with deepening interest the impressive series of meetings throughout the province, which have culminated in this final protest. The same note of sincerity and enthusiasm ran through them all. The impression left on the mind of every competent observer is that of a community absolutely united in its resistance to the act of separation with which it is threatened ... Liberal speakers and writers have tried to persuade English electors, mostly ignorant of the conditions which prevail in Ireland, that the 'Orange' sentiment is largely artificial, and has been manufactured to serve the ends of the Unionist Party. The subscription to the Covenant and the transactions that preceded it are the answer to these allegations ... If there were no other obstacle to Home Rule, that which is embodied in the opposition of Ulster is the rock upon which the Bill must shipwreck in the end. We believe that these Northern gatherings have brought that conviction home to many thousands of Englishmen."

The *Daily Sketch* on 30 September 1912, reporting on Ulster Day. *(PRONI D1261/2579)*

13

THE SEQUEL

ULSTER DAY WAS UNQUESTIONABLY A remarkable triumph as a demonstration of Unionist solidarity and determination. As the culmination of a series of impressive mass demonstrations, it marked the end of the first phase of the Unionist campaign. Since the Liberal Government had already flagrantly violated the spirit of the Constitution by introducing a Home Rule Bill, a vital issue affecting the entire British nation and its Empire, without even the pretence of an electoral mandate, Unionists could no longer rely on the parliamentary path alone. There were things greater than parliamentary majorities when the future of a people was at stake as Bonar Law asserted. This shaped the character of the next phase of the campaign. Posterity would judge the Unionists not on the basis of fine speeches but by their deeds. The time for mere words had passed. There was no longer any substitute for action. The road before them was to lead to the establishment of the Ulster Volunteer Force; the landing of rifles and ammunition at Larne, Bangor and Donaghadee; and the formation of the Provisional Government.

Beyond that lay the Battle of the Somme where:

> "those splendid troops drawn from those volunteers who had banded themselves together for another cause... shed their blood like water for the liberty of the world."

In recognition of their sacrifice, their native Ulster merited special treatment after the Great War: the establishment of the Ulster State. Providence provided Ulster with courageous and inspiring leadership equal to the pre-war crisis.

At the outset, Carson, the hard-headed realist, gave careful consideration to the course upon which the people were about to embark:

> "What I am very anxious about is that the people over there [Ulster] really mean to resist. I am not for a mere game of bluff and unless men are prepared to make great sacrifices which they clearly understand, the talk of resistance is of no use. We will be confronted by many weaklings in our own camp who talk very loud and mean nothing and will be the first to criticise us when the moment of actions comes."

By late 1912 an air of unreality pervaded the Liberal benches in the House of Commons. The realists in the Liberal Party – men such as Lloyd George – privately conceded the force and justice of Ulster's argument, but self-interest ensured that such an admission would never pass their lips in public. Those who shared Asquith's self-delusion smugly believed that the mere passage of the Home Rule Bill three times through the House of Commons would make Dublin rule a reality. It is extremely doubtful that Asquith, the Liberal Imperialist and follower of Lord Rosebery, had any serious commitment to Home Rule. His 'belief' in Home Rule was purely the product of parliamentary arithmetic. His government needed the votes of Irish nationalist MPs to remain in office.

In November 1912, by masterly tactics, the Unionist opposition inflicted a humiliating defeat on the Liberal Government during a crucial Home Rule debate. A

All over Ulster men were drilling yet there was no overall command or structure.
Here men stand to attention outside St John's (Malone) Church of Ireland at night. *(PRONI INF7A/2/23)*

shudder went through the Liberal benches; even Asquith was rattled. They well knew that, with by-election after by-election promising them nothing more than crushing electoral humiliation, they must hold on at all costs. Thus constitutional convention was cast aside, and even the losing of a major Commons vote was argued away as a matter of no consequence.

Amid this highly-charged atmosphere, a leading Liberal realist, Winston Churchill, taunted the Unionist benches. An enraged Ronald McNeill, an Ulster Unionist representing the St Augustine's division of Kent since 1911, gave vent to the feelings of the entire Opposition benches by seizing a small bound copy of the Orders of the House and symbolically throwing it at Churchill. The force of Ulster's argument came home to the offending Liberal with a thump.

Fully aware of the Government's willingness to override the Constitution, unionists were drilling and acquiring military skills even before the signing of the Covenant. County Tyrone Orangemen are traditionally credited, almost certainly erroneously, with leading the way and soon Orange Order leaders all over Ulster were following their example. Such was the measure of their commitment that after a hard day's toil in the fields or the factories, men walked for miles to attend parades and drills. Social distinctions were forgotten. Gentry cheerfully obeyed orders from their tenants and company directors from their employees. For example, in County Down the Seaforde Company included Major William George Forde JP DL, the major local landowner, and his sixteen-year-old son, Thomas William Forde, in its ranks. However, the company was actually commanded by Alexander

Ulster and Parliament. A depiction of a debate inside Westminster from *The Graphic,* 23 November 2012 *(PRONI INF7A/2/53)*

Members of Ballynafeigh and Newtownbreda Unionist Club practising semaphore. *(PRONI INF7A/2/21)*

McMeekin, the Forde's coachman. In Newtownbutler, County Fermanagh, Viscount Crichton, the eldest son of the Earl of Erne, attended drilling in the village but not in a leadership role. However, this may have been to avoid jeopardising his position as equerry to the King and endangering his commission in the Royal Horse Guards.

In the photograph on page 84 a solicitor, a manual worker and a small shopkeeper practise semaphore signalling. While some derided these military preparations, a senior British officer noted that there reigned in Ulster "a stern and disciplined atmosphere and a serious spirit of unity and organisation."

In January 1913, the Ulster Unionist Council decided that the volunteers should be united into a single body to be known as the Ulster Volunteer Force. Recruitment was to be limited to 100,000 men who had signed the Covenant. In urging Unionists to enrol, Carson recognised the importance of organisation and unity:

> "Victory comes to those who are organised and united. Those who are unorganised cannot help and may hinder our efforts."

An organisation similar to that of the recently reorganised Territorial Army was created. An efficient Headquarters staff was set up, which benefited enormously from the expertise of Captain Wilfrid Spender, the youngest staff officer in the British Army, who threw up a promising career to identify himself more closely with Ulster's cause. On the recommendation of Lord Roberts of Kandahar, the most distinguished soldier alive, Lieutenant-General Sir George Richardson, himself a distinguished soldier, was appointed to command the Volunteers.

An impressive array of specialist units which would

WHERE THE AMMUNITION IS KEPT
Ulster Volunteers guarding the Armoury at Craigavon.

NO ADMISSION EXCEPT ON BUSINESS
Refusing permission to the Royal Irish Constabulary.

CRAIGAVON — ULSTER VOLUNTEERS EMPTYING THEIR BANDOLIERS

The formation of the Ulster Volunteer Force. *(PRONI INF7A/3/53)*

Carson and Craig with members of the Signalling and Despatch Riders Corps.
(PRONI INF7A/3/43)

The mobilisation of an entire community made it evident for all to see that Unionists had not been bluffing when they had pledged themselves to "Using all means which may be found necessary" to defeat the imposition of Dublin rule. Like their seventeenth century forefathers they would not allow control of their lives and liberties to be transferred into the hands of their political opponents by a corrupt Liberal Government. Ulster would fight and Ulster would be right.

In the words of the seventeenth century philosopher Thomas Hobbes: "Covenants without swords are but words."

Carson realised that it was not enough to preach the use of force without making practical preparations to acquire the means. The UVF's military effectiveness was seriously impaired by having insufficient weapons and ammunition. A bold stroke was required and by 1914 was essential because according to the terms of the Parliament Act of 1911, which drastically reduced the powers of the Conservative-dominated House of Lords, nothing would stand between Ulster and Dublin rule but armed resistance. With Carson's unequivocal support, Major Frederick Crawford (who had allegedly signed the Covenant in his own blood) in a daring mission travelled to Germany, purchased guns and ammunition and brought them safely to Ulster. On the night of 24/25 April 35,000 rifles and 3,000,000 rounds of ammunition were successfully unloaded at Larne, Bangor and Donaghadee, and swiftly and efficiently distributed to the UVF right across the Province. Ulster unionists now not only had the will but also the means to oppose the imposition of Dublin rule.

As early as September 1911, at the great Craigavon Demonstration, Carson told the assembled multitudes:

have been the envy of many a contemporary professional army were established; the Special Services Sections, the Medical Corps, the Nursing Corps and the Signalling and Despatch Riders Corps. The UVF's finest despatch rider was Godfrey Boyton of Convoy, County Donegal. The son of the Dean of Derry, Boyton was the winner of the Isle of Man Tourist Trophy in 1913.

It was not only the men of Ulster who responded magnificently to the call; women came forward not only as nurses but as signallers, motor-cycle despatch riders and ambulance drivers. At UVF Headquarters a small group was engaged in intelligence work which included the deciphering of intercepted police messages.

The Gunrunners aboard the *Fanny* in the Kiel Canal. *(PRONI D961/3/002)*

Back row: Fred Crawford (the UVF's Director of Ordnance), Captain Andrew Agnew (of the Antrim Iron Ore Steamship Company and captain of the *Fanny*) and Bruno Spiro (the Berlin gunsmith from whom the guns were purchased).

Front Row: Captain Marthin Falck (the Norwegian captain and former owner of the *Fanny*) and Helen Crawford (Fred Crawford's wife).

A lorry being loaded at Donaghadee from a lighter which had transferred guns and ammunition from the SS *Clyde Valley* at Larne. *(Private Collection)*

James Craig commanded the operation at Donaghadee and can clearly be seen in the centre of the photograph. *(Private Collection)*

"We must be prepared ... the morning Home Rule passes, ourselves to become responsible for the government of the Protestant province of Ulster."

Exactly two years later the Ulster Unionist Council approved the setting up of a Provisional Government if Home Rule should become law and delegating its powers to a Provisional Government with Carson at its head. A military council was established and sub-committees were created with comprehensive responsibility for all the various functions of government.

On 9 July 1914, as the Home Rule Bill neared the statute book, James Craig released the text of the preamble and some of the articles of the constitution of the Provisional Government. The administration of Ulster was to be taken over:

"in trust for the constitution of the United Kingdom [and] upon the restoration of direct Imperial Government, the Provisional Government shall cease to exist."

Five days later, in a speech to a closed meeting of the Ulster Unionist Council, Carson explained the gravity of the situation. An account of the proceedings on that momentous day has been preserved for posterity by Ronald McNeill, an Ulster Unionist representing an English constituency and author of *Ulster's Stand for Union* (1922):

"Nothing remained for them in Ulster but to carry out the policy they had resolved upon long ago, and make good the Covenant ... The course to be followed in assuming the administration was explained and agreed to, and when they separated all the members felt that the crisis for which they had been preparing so long had at last come upon them. There was no flinching."

The principal members of the Provisional Government of Ulster. *(Grand Orange Lodge of Ireland)*

Front Row (left to right): William Moore, MP; Lord Dunleath; Lord Londonderry; Sir Edward Carson; Duke of Abercorn; Sir John Lonsdale, MP.

In the second row (selected): Godfrey Featherstonhaugh, MP; HT Barrie, MP; Capt James Craig, MP; Gen Sir George Richardson; WJ MacGeagh MacCaw, MP; Col Hacket Pain; Capt The Hon Arthur O'Neill, MP.

However events in Europe soon overtook them and the Great War intervened. At the outbreak of war in August 1914 it was no surprise that the newly appointed Minister of War, Lord Kitchener, cast covetous eyes on a well-armed UVF created to fight Home Rule. Asked by Kitchener to provide four battalions, Sir Edward Carson offered a division of 12 battalions, uniformed and equipped at Ulster's expense. Carson declared:

> "England's difficulty is not Ulster's opportunity. However we are treated, and however others act, let us act rightly. We do not seek to purchase terms by selling our patriotism."

Thus the UVF became the 36th (Ulster) Division. On

Charge of the 36th (Ulster) Division, Somme, 1 July 1916 by James Prinsep Beadle RA. *(Courtesy Belfast City Council)*

1st July 1916 the men of the Ulster Division distinguished themselves with courage and heroism during the opening of the Allied offensive on the Somme. On that day four members of the Division won Victoria Crosses. Observing the charge of the Ulster Division, Captain (later Lieutenant Colonel Sir) Wilfrid Spender commenced his famous account with the following words:

"I am not an Ulsterman but yesterday … as I followed their amazing attack I felt I would rather be an Ulsterman than anything else in the world."

The final sentences of Spender's eye-witness account

may serve as a tribute to the devotion and sacrifice of the Division:

> "The Ulster Division has lost more than half the men who attacked and, in doing so, has sacrificed itself for the Empire which has treated them none too well. The much derided Ulster Volunteer Force has won a name which equals any in history. Their devotion, which no doubt has helped the advance elsewhere, deserved the gratitude of the British Empire. It is due to the memory of these brave fellows that their beloved Province shall be fairly treated."

The painting opposite depicts the 11th Battalion of the Royal Irish Rifles (South Antrim Volunteers), the Right Forward Unit of the 108th Infantry Brigade. The young officer with arm raised is Lieutenant Francis Bodenham Thornley, who was one month short of his 20th birthday on 1 July 1916. During the battle he was wounded and while recuperating was assigned to assist Beadle produce this painting.

James Prinsep Beadle was principally known as a painter of historical and military subjects, which might be considered appropriate for the son of Major General James P Beadle RE.

The painting was exhibited at the Royal Academy in 1917 and was later presented to the Corporation of the City of Belfast. The painting was officially unveiled here on 1 July 1918, by the Lady Mayoress and accepted by the Lord Mayor (Alderman James Johnston) on behalf of the corporation.

After the Great War, Ulster did receive special treatment but ironically the terms of the Government of Ireland Act (1920) foisted Home Rule on the one part of Ireland which abhorred constitutional experiment. Sir James Craig, Ulster's first Prime Minister, accurately reflected the Ulster Unionist position:

> "As a final settlement and supreme sacrifice in the interests of peace the Government of Ireland Act was accepted by Northern Ireland, although not asked for by her representatives."

Despite this imposed and unwelcome settlement, Craig and his colleagues set about the formidable task of creating and moulding the destiny of the new State. Again they benefited from the organisational abilities of those men who had led the Covenant campaign before the War. As Craig recognised:

> "When later on, we look back upon this very engaging and interesting chapter of Ulster history... I at all events will be able to stand over every appointment I have made, and thank God every day I had such talent to choose from."

The State that was thus born was born of a sense of victory. Ulster had faced not only the combined and powerful forces of Irish Nationalism and English Liberalism, had not only defied a corrupt and unscrupulous Government but had also run the very risk of its ultimate extinction as part of the United Kingdom. Against these overwhelming odds, the grim determination and resolution, the inspired leadership, the unshakeable unity and disciplined organisation of Unionism had ensured the state's future. Ulster remained British.

ACKNOWLEDGEMENTS

MOST OF THE IMAGES REPRODUCED in this book are in the Public Record Office of Northern Ireland and, more specifically, in the archive of the Ulster Unionist Council. We are deeply indebted to the Deputy Keeper of Records and her staff for their invaluable assistance.

We would also wish to express our thanks to the following individuals and institutions:

Paul Abraham
David Bushe
E Creighton
Gemma Eaton
John Erskine
Ian Hamilton
Bobby Hanvey
Dr David Hume MBE
Mrs Mack
Ian Montgomery
Dr Bethany Sinclair
Nora Totten
Michael Treanor

Belfast Central Library
Belfast City Council
Grand Orange Lodge of Ireland
Linen Hall Library
Schomberg House
Ulster Unionist Party

INDEX

Page numbers in **bold** indicate illustrations.